Governing the Police

Governing
the Police

Experience in
Six Democracies

David H. Bayley
and
Philip C. Stenning

Transaction Publishers
New Brunswick (U.S.A.) and London (U.K.)

Library of Congress Catalog Number: 2015047582
ISBN: 978-1-4128-6281-3 (hardcover); 978-1-4128-6338-4 (paperback)
eBook: 978-1-4128-6231-8
Printed in the United States of America

Library of Congress Cataloging-in-Publication Data

Names: Bayley, David H., author. | Stenning, Philip C.
Title: Governing the police : experience in six democratic countries / by David H. Bayley and Philip C. Stenning.
Description: New Brunswick (USA) : Transaction Publishers, 2016. | Includes bibliographical references and index.
Identifiers: LCCN 2015047582 (print) | LCCN 2016004489 (ebook) | ISBN 9781412862813 (hardcover) | ISBN 9781412862318 (eBook) | ISBN 9781412862318 (eBook)
Subjects: LCSH: Police..
Classification: LCC HV7921 .B353 2016 (print) | LCC HV7921 (ebook) | DDC 353.3/6–dc23
LC record available at http://lccn.loc.gov/

2015047582

To my daughters Jennifer and Tracy, for their love, understanding, and good sense.

David H. Bayley

In memory of my early mentor, the late Professor John Edwards (1918-1994), who inspired me to pursue an academic career, and instilled in me values which have guided me throughout it.

Philip C. Stenning

Contents

Acknowledgments

This book could not have been written without the generous co-operation of senior police officers, both serving and retired, in Australia, Britain, Canada, India, New Zealand, and the United States. To say they were interested in the topic would be an understatement. Uniformly they stressed the importance of managing their relationship with political supervisors. They all had stories to tell, not necessarily critical. For their insights, candor, and willingness to be interviewed, as well as their assistance in putting us in touch with other members of their elite group who agreed to be interviewed, we are enormously grateful.

We are indebted for the support we have received from the following institutions: the School of Criminal Justice and its Hindelang Criminal Justice Research Center, State University of New York at Albany, NY; the School of Criminology and Criminal Justice, Griffith University, Queensland, Australia; the Australian Institute of Police Management at Manly, New South Wales; the Institute of Criminology at Victoria University of Wellington, New Zealand; and the Australian Institute of Criminology in Canberra, Australian Capital Territory.

We owe a special debt to the School of Criminology and Criminal Justice at Griffith University for providing two opportunities for the authors to meet in Brisbane over several weeks to plan and discuss the book. Without these meetings, the book would have been difficult to write.

In preparing the book for publication we received expert help from Kathleen Maguire, former editor of the Sourcebook on Criminal Justice Statistics, School of Criminal Justice, Albany, NY. She was a delightful collaborator in this enterprise. We are also most grateful to Ms. Mary Curtis and Mr. Jeffrey Stetz of Transaction Publishers for all their encouragement, co-operation, and assistance in shepherding the book through the publication process.

Writing a book is absorbing to its authors, but often obscure and sometimes burdensome to their friends and family. For their unqualified, if puzzled, understanding throughout, we are grateful.

1

A Democratic Dilemma

Every democracy confronts a fundamental problem: how can elected governments create and manage police so that they act in the public interest while avoiding the temptation to use them for their own partisan advantage? This book examines how six English-speaking democracies are dealing with this problem. It describes how frequently disagreements arise between supervising politicians and operational police commanders, what issues are involved, and how they are resolved. The book focuses particularly on the daily, informal interactions between politicians and police as they balance their respective obligations. By studying the problem comparatively among countries, the book assesses the factors that help to manage the relationship in the public interest.

In this book, we examine government's relations with the public police—police that are created, supported, and directed by government. These are the police that the public relies on to respond to emergencies, control disorder, and investigate crime. Their senior commanders have various titles: chief, commissioner, chief constable, superintendent, chief superintendent, director, and director-general. For simplicity, we will refer to all of them as "chiefs."

In democratic countries, police are accountable to government; politicians have ultimate responsibility. At the same time, politicians can misuse the police. Their oversight can be inept, abusive, illegal, and partisan. The democratic dilemma is to ensure that elected governments hold the police to public account while not at the same time abusing their authority. The dilemma has been described in various ways—political control versus operational independence, accountability versus professionalism, and policy formulation versus operational implementation. However described, getting the balance right is not easy, particularly because it depends on changes in circumstances, political as well as social, that cannot always be foreseen.

We will examine the balance between political accountability and understandings of police independence in six English-speaking democracies—Australia, Britain, Canada, India, New Zealand, and the United States. In addition to being democratic, these countries have legal systems based on the Common Law and all, except obviously one, have been British colonies. India is the most different in two respects: it does not have a developed economy and, although crime is officially reported as relatively low, only it is experiencing persistent, organized violence directed against government and the police.

Including "Britain" raises an important terminology issue. The United Kingdom comprises England, Wales, Scotland, and Northern Ireland. It is often referred to incorrectly as Great Britain or even more simply as Britain. By and large, the laws, forms of government, and customs are similar throughout. There are, however, important differences currently between England and Wales, on the one hand, and Scotland and Northern Ireland, on the other. Since we interviewed police chiefs only in England and Wales, our use of the term "Britain" in this book refers only to England and Wales, and not to the other elements of the United Kingdom.

With respect to police governance, Britain presents a difficulty as well as a unique opportunity. In 2011 the system of police governance changed radically in England and Wales. The local Police Authorities, which were part of the so-called "tripartite" police governance system consisting of Police Authorities, Home Secretary, and chief constables, were replaced by directly elected local Police and Crime Commissioners. Thus Britain offers an opportunity for before-and-after observation of a planned and very significant change in police governance. We will refer to the current system as "new" Britain and the one that was superseded as "old" Britain. While the information about "old" Britain is extensive, information about "new" Britain is not. Because the change of governance is so recent, we are unable to say anything definitive about its impact. None of our other five countries has experienced a similarly radical transformation in police governance in recent years.

With one exception, police in our sample are organized at several levels of government—national, state/provincial, regional, and municipal. Only New Zealand has a single centralized police system, therefore a single "chief" interacting with the government. In the other countries a direct political–police relationship occurs at all levels. We have chosen not to investigate the governance of national police agencies unless those agencies also do street patrols and respond to calls-for-service from the public, that is, provide services to individuals rather than exclusively to government, as, for example, the FBI in the United States and the Central Bureau of Investigation in India. We have, however, included the Australian Federal Police (AFP) and the Royal Canadian Mounted Police (RCMP). The AFP serves as the law enforcement arm of the Australian government but also bears primary responsibility for public safety in Canberra, the Australian Capital Territory. The RCMP assumes responsibility for general-duties policing under contractual agreements in eight of the ten provinces and in several municipalities.

The book does not examine all the disagreements that may arise between politicians and chiefs. We focus on a particular subset, namely, where they disagree about who's in charge. Specifically, where politicians try to direct the police in ways they should not, where police defend their operational prerogative, and where police claim too much independence and try to evade legitimate oversight and political accountability. More broadly, we are interested in whether there are principles of law or custom that limit disputes or whether politicians and police chiefs negotiate the balance again and again according to their own convenience and understanding.

Our analysis draws on many sources of information—scholarly writing, official reports, legal opinions, media sources, legislative and other public inquiries, judicial decisions, memoirs, biographies, job advertisements and descriptions, employment contracts, conference reports, and orders from governments. Major writing on the political–police relation is reviewed in detail in chapter 3. Our book's unique contribution to this writing is to examine police governance as experienced by police chiefs and to do so comparatively among a sample of democratic countries.

As part of the research for this book, we conducted personal interviews with senior police executives (mostly chiefs), both serving and retired, in each of the six democratic countries. We did this in order to explore in practical detail the nature of the governance relationship, to get at the nitty-gritty of what was being asked, what was resisted or resented, what was at stake, what process was followed, and who blinked. We conducted over 100 interviews covering all six countries. They were not, however, a scientific sampling. In countries with only a few police forces, such as New Zealand and Australia, we could cover most. That would have been difficult to do in the countries with many police jurisdictions, such as Canada with either 179 or 480, depending on how one counts, and the United States with over 17,000. The Canadian discrepancy is explained in chapter 4. In these countries, we tried to sample experience in police departments that differed in regional location, size, and governance structure. We interviewed on the basis of a "convenience sample," utilizing professional contacts, friendships, and referrals from one official to another. Once we were satisfied in the rough representativeness of our coverage, we interviewed in each country until we were hearing the same things again and again.

The interviews in New Zealand were undertaken in 2004–06, and included former police commissioners who had served in that position between 1978 and 2000. The interviews in the other five countries were undertaken between 2012 and 2014. They too included chiefs who had served during the preceding twenty years.[1]

All interviews were undertaken with a pledge of confidentiality. Accordingly, we have neither listed the names of the people interviewed nor attributed information to named interviewees without permission. As one chief wryly remarked, "You mean I've got to talk to you and I don't get any credit for it?"

Because our interviews do not come from comparable samples, we have not analyzed them statistically to determine differences in experience either between or within countries. We have used the interview information to illuminate what goes on in the give-and-take of police governance.

In the end, our conclusions reflect a synthesis of scholarship, observations, and interviews collected over our lifetimes of study. They are the result of "triangulation" among sources, hoping that the weaknesses of each will be compensated by their collective range. Our analysis produces informed conjectures rather than tested findings. We submit them in the hope that they will encourage others to undertake further comparative studies of this important topic.

Regardless of methodology, there is an unavoidable obstacle to assessing the extent of either excessive political intrusion or failures of accountability. Detecting these twin defects in police governance depends upon one of the parties protesting what is occurring and making it visible. If the police accommodate overreaching direction by politicians or politicians accept police explanations for not informing, there is no visible foul. The protagonists themselves may not even be conscious of one. In other words, absent detailed bright lines in legislation, judicial precedent, or executive rule, the visibility of problems in the relationship between politicians and police depends entirely on the perceptions of the protagonists. Moreover, by failing to protest, the accommodating official becomes complicit. Either they recognized the problem and did not protest or they did and conceded for reasons of expediency. In both cases they would be reluctant to admit they had not lived up to their responsibility.

Since accommodation makes both parties complicit, it is hard to determine confidently whether governance is working in the public interest. This hampers any third-party investigation—legal processes, independent inquiries, investigative journalism, and interviews with participants. Conclusions about the quality of police governance have as much to do with what becomes visible as with the amount of substantive disagreement.

This also suggests that the testimony of participants to the quality of their relations depends to some extent upon political/managerial cultures. Since these evolve over time, it means that across both time and space the ways in which politicians and police chiefs behave may not change but assessments of what is acceptable may.

Another limitation of our study is that we did not try to balance our interviews with police with the perceptions of supervising politicians. We did not for several reasons. Surveying politicians would have required considerably more time and funding. Furthermore, in countries where there are only a few police jurisdictions, such as New Zealand, Australia, and Britain, interviewing politicians would create a "diplomatic" problem. We would inevitably hear stories where both players, knowing the other was being interviewed, would want us to "get it right." This could inhibit frankness, increase self-justification, and undermine confidence in our pledge of confidentiality.

The fact is that we are not interested so much in the "right" of particular events as in the experience of conflict. We present the police perspective. Their narrative is admittedly only half the story. Like all of us, they want to appear in a favorable light. As a result, they characteristically represent themselves as victims or heroes. We have no examples of chiefs who said, in effect, "I really screwed up." We hope that other scholars will provide the politicians' narratives and compare them with what we report from police chiefs.

Relying largely on police testimony, as we have done, suggests a question that scholars who study politicians in police governance might address: Are police chiefs and politicians equally sensitive to the "balance" in the relationship? For chiefs, defending their prerogatives is a central issue. Perhaps because police are in the subordinate position, they may be more attentive to the governance relationship. Politicians, on the other hand, have a wider ambit of responsibility. They have other things to do than ensure that the police are responsive and accountable. Furthermore, their responsibility for policing is often quite brief, being a stage in a broader political career. They will often have little experience or expertise with respect to policing when appointed.

By contrast, for police chiefs, policing is their career. It may be, therefore, that police are more likely to feel the constraint of interference than politicians are to feel the lack of account-ability. In short, when it comes to assessing the health of the police~governance relationship, police executives may be the canary in the coal mine, with the important difference that when the conditions deteriorate they do not keel over but squawk louder.

This is not to suggest that politicians and police executives are always struggling for dominance. Politicians are often delighted to delegate responsibility for public safety to the police, just as police executives often recognize that being accountable to representative public opinion is critically important to their image and their effectiveness. The rela-tionship between politicians and chiefs is often collaborative, based on a comfortable agreement that both accountability and independence are needed and that they have achieved the proper balance.

To summarize, the purpose of this book is to compare the practice and culture of police governance in six contemporary English-speaking democracies. What are the institutions, understandings, and practices at the point of interaction between elected politicians and police commanders?

The book is organized into three parts: Part I presents the intellectual and institutional context of police governance; part II, the practice of police governance; and part III, a re-examination of contemporary police governance. In part I, chapter 2 provides examples of some of the most visible and serious disagreements about police governance from each country. Chapter 3 reviews the evolution of scholarship about police governance. Chapter 4 describes the current police-governance structures in each country and the gov-ernmental and social structures ("settings") within which they operate.

Part II describes the police–political interaction in the six countries based largely, but not exclusively, on interviews with chiefs. Chapter 5 discusses the frequency with which disagreements occur, the issues that are involved, the process of disagreement, and the results. Chapter 6 presents advice from police chiefs about how to minimize and manage disagreements.

In part III, we discuss what we have learned about the management of police governance. Chapter 7 explains the reasons for serious disagreement between politicians and police chiefs. Chapter 8 describes the evolving context of police governance. Chapter 9 reviews mechanisms for managing the police–government relationship and presents our conclusions about improving the management of the democratic dilemma.

Note

1. The Australian Institute of Criminology also kindly gave us access to recordings of nine interviews with commissioners and former commissioners that it had commissioned in 1999 and 2000.

Part I

Contexts

2

When Things Go Wrong

The premise of this study is that there is inevitable tension in democratic countries over the governance of the police between chiefs and their political supervisors. It is generated by competing views about the balance between accountability and independence. Considering the number of interactions between chiefs and their political bosses, the relationship most of the time is harmonious, or at least workable. Occasionally, however, it goes dramatically wrong. Either the politician or the police chief confronts a demand he or she cannot accept. For police, it may be an order they perceive as intruding on their professional autonomy; for politicians, it is a refusal by police to inform and explain or comply with their directives. Although accommodation by one or the other is the most common outcome, agreement sometimes becomes impossible, leading to resignations, dismissals or non-renewal of contracts, public charges and countercharges, and avid commentary by the news media. In this chapter, we present examples of how bad things can get when the police–government relationship breaks down.

Our descriptions are not evenhanded in the sense of representing the views of both parties. We have not tried to assess respective responsibilities. We report what the dispute looked like on the basis of public charge and countercharge. Our descriptions are also weighted in favor of police accounts because we have interviewed only chiefs and not politicians. Wherever we could, we have cited the findings of official inquiries. In this chapter, we describe particularly egregious examples from each of the six countries we studied. They are not presented as representative of all chief-political supervisor disputes either in our six countries or in other democracies.

Australia

Case One: "Meddling" Politicians

Between the 1970s and 1990s, the New South Wales Police Service was the subject of numerous allegations of corruption and inefficiency. It was a tough time for the Service's police commissioners as well as for the NSW government, each of whom found themselves publicly blamed for this situation, and for their failure to "deal with it." Both police commissioners and police ministers desperately tried to convince the media, parliamentarians, and the public that they were aggressively addressing these concerns. As a result, the boundary lines between the respective responsibilities and authority of the police ministers and the commissioners became increasingly blurred.

In 1981, the presumed "ground rules" for the police minister/police commissioner relationship had been the subject of recommendations in the report of a commission of inquiry which had been set up to look into the administration of the police service. Mr. Justice Lusher, who chaired the commission, had concluded that the relationship required both an improved oversight capacity for the minister and a greater degree of distance in order to reduce the likelihood of improper political interference in the administration of the force (New South Wales, Commission to Inquire, 1981, 789). To achieve this, he recommended the establishment of a three-member police board, to be interposed as a governing body between the minister and the police service. This recommendation was implemented two years later. The membership of the Board consisted of two government appointees, one of whom (the Chair) was a former corporate CEO from the private sector, and the other the police commissioner. Lusher had spelled out in some detail what the relationships between the minister, the Police Board, and the commissioner should be, in terms of the governance of the police service.

Right after the Lusher report was made public, the Police Commissioner, Mr. John Avery, retired, having served in the office for seven years. Although this was publicly presented as a normal retirement, some senior officers, including Avery's immediate successor as commissioner, suggested to a subsequent parliamentary inquiry that Avery had decided to retire early as a result of "tensions" between him and the Police Minister, Mr. Ted Pickering. While Avery confirmed in his testimony to the inquiry that there had been occasional tensions, he did not confirm that these had precipitated his decision to retire (Duncan, 1993, 198–204). His departure, of course, necessitated the appointment of a new commissioner. His former Deputy Commissioner, Mr. Tony Lauer, was appointed.

Between the time Avery retired and Lauer took office, the minister relocated his offices to the top floor of the police headquarters building, which had up to then been the offices of the police commissioner. The commissioner's offices were relocated to two floors below the minister's, with the Police Board's offices located on the floor in between. The symbolism of this was not lost on the police service.

Commissioner Lauer served under Minister Pickering for less than two years, during which their relationship progressively deteriorated. The commissioner felt that the minister was constantly and excessively interfering in matters of the administration of the police service that were his or the Police Board's responsibility, while the minister for his part felt that the commissioner had on a few occasions inappropriately intervened in discussions of government policy (e.g., with respect to gun licensing), which were his responsibility as minister, and had not accounted to him truthfully about certain police operations. The subsequent parliamentary inquiry into the breakdown of this relationship described it as having involved a "series of occurrences which put great strains on the relationship, culminating in its total breakdown. Some of these incidents appear on the surface to be of little consequence. However, seen as a sequence, each assumes significance" (Duncan, 1993, 195). The report states that by eighteen months after Lauer assumed office:

> There were now intractable differences between Commissioner Lauer and Mr. Pickering. These were both personal and professional. It is apparent that their relationship had reached such a low ebb by this point that it was only a matter of time before some issues arose which would cause an 'irretrievable breakdown'. (p. 293).

The final breakdown in their relationship was precipitated by a dispute between the minister and the commissioner as to whether the commissioner had kept the minister informed, in a timely fashion, about a high-profile incident involving the attempted suicide of a teenager in a police station. The matter had been the subject of a current affairs television program several months after it had occurred, and in answer to Opposition questions about it in Parliament, the minister had stated that he had not been informed about it by the police service at the time, and had first heard about it as a result of the television broadcast. The commissioner, who was away from Sydney visiting a rural police station at the time, told journalists that the minister was mistaken and that he had papers that demonstrated that the minister had been informed about the incident months before. The minister was accused of having misled parliament, as a result of which he was relieved of the police portfolio by the Premier.

This is a rare example where the minister rather than the commissioner was the "fall guy." The case is documented in extraordinary detail in the reports of the Joint Select Committee of the New South Wales Parliament that inquired into the circumstances leading to the minister's resignation. The report concluded that Lauer also bore considerable responsibility for the breakdown of the relationship, but concluded that this was not such as would justify a call for him to resign. But more was to come.

Lauer remained in office as the commissioner for another three years. During those years there were a growing number of allegations of ongoing corruption within the Police Service. Early on, however, Lauer publicly dismissed these, saying that this problem was "historic" and had been satisfactorily addressed. The Government, however, did not agree, and in 1994 set up a Royal Commission to look into these allegations. Lauer came under heavy criticism, including calls for his resignation, in the media and in parliament for his denial that there was a problem, and less than a year after the Commission began its hearings, he resigned at the age of sixty, after five years in office and well before the end date of his latest contract. The commissioner's departure was presented once again as a voluntary retirement despite the fact that there were strong suspicions that this was not the case and that he had been encouraged to quit by an embarrassed government.[1]

Case Two: Partisan Contamination

The full circumstances surrounding the resignation in June 2011 of Simon Overland as Chief Commissioner of the State of Victoria Police, after just over two years in the job, are too complex to recount in detail. In what follows, we highlight one critical aspect of them—that he was perceived to be "too close" to the Labour Party that was in government in Victoria at the time of his appointment in 2009 and throughout most of his short tenure as chief commissioner. This perception may well have been in circulation before his appointment, but particular events at the ceremony of his investiture—that the Premier and the police minister personally pinned the Chief Commissioner epaulets to his uniform—were subsequently cited by many as indicative of the truth of the perception (Munro 2011).

Overland served most of his police career (nineteen years) in the Australian Federal Police (AFP) before joining Victoria Police as an assistant commissioner in 2003, when Christine Nixon was serving as Australia's first female police commissioner. In 2006 he was promoted to deputy commissioner. By the time he was appointed chief commissioner, therefore, he had served in the Victoria Police for six years. During those years, and until the end of 2010, the Labour Party was in power in the State.

Overland's brief spell as chief commissioner was plagued with controversy, but two events in particular seem to have accounted for his decision to resign in 2011. The first was the electoral defeat of the State Labour Government in December 2010. The second was an allegation, which surfaced after the election, that immediately prior to the election period, Overland had authorized the release of "unsettled" crime statistics which the government was able to use to political advantage in its election campaign (Brouwer, 2011, 7). This allegation became the subject of an investigation by the

Victorian Ombudsman, whose report on the matter was highly critical of Overland. The Ombudsman concluded that "The decision to release the crime statistics several days before the caretaker period was the Chief Commissioner's, and his alone"; "the figure of 27.5 per cent reduction [in the number of assaults in the Melbourne CBD] was misleading and inconsistent with all other available data"; and "The release of the quarterly crime statistics data, particularly so close to an election, was likely to be used in a political context," and had in fact been so used by the police minister in an election debate with the Opposition police spokesman (Brouwer 2011, 28–29).

After reading the Ombudsman's report, and before its public release, the new police minister consulted with the Premier. The minister subsequently stated that as a result of this consultation "The Government concluded that the report presented issues in relation to the management of Victoria Police that were of serious concern." He then "spoke with the Chief Commissioner and advised him of the Government's concerns."[2] He said that during this discussion Overland had "indicated his intention to submit his resignation" and that in light of this "we reached mutual agreement with him" (Levy 2011). At his press conference the following day, confirming his resignation, Overland insisted that he "wasn't pushed" and that the Ombudsman's report was not "the final straw" that caused him to resign. Rather, he said, there had been "a lot of distractions over the last little while" which did not seem likely to abate, and that in these circumstances he believed that it was "in the best interests of Victoria and Victoria Police for me to leave" (Levy 2011).

In October 2011, an Office of Police Integrity (OPI) report concluded that the police minister's ministerial adviser and his parliamentary secretary had conspired with Overland's deputy commissioner to get Overland fired or forced to resign, and that the minister had not been informed of their involvement. As a result, both of them resigned. In March 2013, however, secretly recorded tapes were released which suggested that the minister had lied to the OPI, and that he had in fact been informed of their contacts with the deputy commissioner. The tapes also revealed that the Premier's Chief of Staff and the Liberal Party's state director had known about this (Ferguson 2014). As a result, the Premier resigned and the police minister was "shuffled" to a new portfolio by the new Premier. The Labour Party indicated that if elected in elections in November 2014, it would ask the new Independent Broad-Based Anti-Corruption Commission (IBAC) to conduct a full investigation into the whole matter (Ferguson 2013). The Labour Party did win the election, but at the time of writing had not referred the matter to IBAC.

Britain

The British cases occurred before 2011 when the new Police and Crime Commissioner System replaced the previous local Police Authorities. Thus these cases are about what we are calling "Old Britain."

Case One: Alleged Partisanship

Our account of the circumstances leading to the resignation of Metropolitan London Police Commissioner Sir Ian Blair in 2008 focuses on one critical aspect of those circumstances— the fact that Blair was perceived to have been "too close" to the Labour Government which had appointed him, and the fact that his resignation was precipitated by pressure from the Conservative Mayor of London in what was widely perceived to be a partisan political move.

From the inception of the Metropolitan Police (commonly referred to as "the Met") in 1829 until the end of the twentieth century, its commissioners were appointed by, and politically exclusively accountable to, the national government, via the Home Secretary. This was because in addition to its local (London) policing responsibilities, the Met had national ones as well. In 1999 legislation established a Police Authority for the governance of the Met, which consisted of a majority of locally elected politicians and was chaired by the elected Mayor of London or his or her designate. From then on, therefore, the commissioner of the Met had two "masters"—the Home Secretary and the mayor—although the former still has exclusive authority with respect to the appointment and dismissal of the commissioner.

When Blair was appointed as commissioner in 2005 for a term of five years, the Home Secretary was part of a Labour Government and the mayor was a Labour politician. In 2008 this changed with the election of Boris Johnson, a Conservative politician, as Mayor of London, and Blair found himself serving under two "masters" of different political stripes. The day after Johnson assumed the chairmanship of the Metropolitan Police Authority, he met with Blair and told him that he did not have confidence in Blair as commissioner and that "he wished there to be a change of leadership at the Met" (Telegraph.co.uk 2008). He apparently had not consulted either the Home Secretary or the Police Authority before this meeting. Later that day Blair tendered his resignation to the Home Secretary who "reluctantly, but graciously, accepted" it (Telegraph.co.uk 2008). He explained his decision to resign in the following terms:

> I am resigning not because of any failures by my Service and not because of the pressures of the office and the many stories that surround it are too much. I am resigning in the best interests of the people of London and of the Metropolitan Police Service. I would have wished to continue to serve Londoners until my time of office expired in

February 2010. However, at a meeting (on Thursday), the new Mayor made clear, in a very pleasant but determined way, that he wished there to be a change of leadership at the Met.

I understand that to serve effectively the Commissioner must have the confidence of both the Mayor and the Home Secretary. Without the Mayor's backing, I do not consider that I can continue in the job. (Telegraph.co.uk 2008)

Although the mayor insisted at the time that his move against Blair had not been politically motivated (Laville and Dodd 2008), it was alleged that when Blair had suggested to him that he should stay in office until a successor had been found, the Mayor had replied that "We don't want a successor appointed. We will have an acting arrangement until a Conservative Home Secretary arrives" (Laville and Norton-Taylor 2008). Johnson declined to disclose the substance of his discussion with Blair, saying that to do so "would be wrong and unfair to Sir Ian" (Laville and Dodd 2008). He was reported in the press, however, to have written a letter to the Home Secretary following the resignation, proposing that he be involved in the selection of Blair's successor, and as having advised the Home Secretary: "I would . . . counsel caution in moving too quickly to recommending a prospective post holder," and that the Home Secretary should "consider whether a fairly lengthy consolidation period, under the acting command of [Deputy Commissioner] Sir Paul Stephenson, might not be for the best" (Laville and Dodd 2008).

Blair's years as commissioner had been plagued with controversy (Laville 2008), and there had been several reasons for people to argue that he had been "too close" to the Labour Government or, as one commentator had described him, "Labour's favourite copper" (Edwards 2008). He had publicly supported the Labour Government's controversial and eventually unsuccessful ninety-day antiterrorist detention proposal during a general election campaign (Silverman 2005), and subsequently "stepped back" from personal involvement in the Met's "Cash for Honours" investigation, citing his "close working relationship with the Prime Minister particularly over security issues" and the need "to ensure that his officers could conduct the investigation without any appearance of conflict of interest" (Hencke 2006). On the other side of the argument, some commentators drew attention to the fact that while the Home Secretary could easily have refused to accept Blair's resignation, she did not, and have suggested that this was because Blair had reached a point at which the Labour Government had come to see him as a political liability and were happy to let Johnson cause him to resign (Porter 2008). Blair himself later insisted that "while admiring his namesake's [Prime Minister Tony Blair] commitment to tackling crime, he was never a paid-up supporter," and argued that if he had been allowed to continue in office he would have "served Boris [Johnson] and served him well," adding:

> It would be fair to say that I'm on the liberal side of policing rather than the hang 'em and flog 'em side. To the extent that one party is closer to that idea than others, then I can see some people saying, 'I don't like this bloke, he's too liberal.' But that doesn't make me a card-carrying Labour member. I was the deputy commissioner and then commissioner for almost 10 years, during which time the party in power was the Labour Party. They had the political mandate. When Boris came in, he specifically asked me to do three things that were in his manifesto. Those three things were done in a matter of weeks, and I didn't see any reports or complaints that I was too close to the Conservatives. (Moss 2009)

It may be that other concerns about Blair's performance would eventually have led to his termination as commissioner. But the evidence suggests strongly that it was the perception of him as "a Labour man" that constituted the principal motive for the Conservative mayor to engineer his demise.

Case Two: Caught in the Cross Fire

The most well-known disputes between chief constables and their local Police Authorities in England in recent times occurred during the highly controversial miners' strike in 1984, during Margaret Thatcher's term as Britain's Conservative Prime Minister. Thatcher was determined to break the strike and her government asserted strong direction in co-ordinating the response of Britain's police forces, on grounds of protecting the "national interest." Much of the "action" during the strike occurred in South Yorkshire, where there were numerous coal mines and a coking plant at Orgreave that became a focus of the miners' mass pickets. The Chief Constable of South Yorkshire, Peter Wright, deployed his police forcefully against the miners, much to the displeasure of the local elected, Labour-controlled South Yorkshire County Council and South Yorkshire Police Authority, which supported the miners and condemned Wright's deployment of the police against them. Ostensibly on grounds of "financial considerations," the Police Authority ordered Wright to disband the force's Mounted Police Unit, which had been deployed effectively against the striking miners, and was a source of much grievance. Wright refused to obey this order, and successfully took the matter to the High Court for an injunction against the Police Authority on the ground that the order was an unlawful attempt to encroach on his operational independence, and was beyond the authority's jurisdiction (Reiner 1991, 194–195).

It was not until thirty years later that it was revealed that the Chief Constable had had the direct backing of the government (specifically the Prime Minister, the Home Secretary, and the Attorney General) in his dispute with his local Police Authority (Jones 2014). This case shows that Britain's "tripartite" police governance arrangements could sometimes be severely strained.

Canada

Case One: Accountability Failure

Giuliano Zaccardelli was appointed as the twentieth commissioner of the Royal Canadian Mounted Police (RCMP) in September 2000, a year before the "9/11" terrorist attack in the United States. The circumstances of his resignation six years later are one of the more bizarre instances of a total police-government relationship breakdown (Stenning 2008). His tenure as commissioner had been punctuated by a number of situations for which he and the RCMP drew strong criticism. But although many of these had led to Opposition calls for his resignation, all three governments under which he had served had continued to publicly express their confidence in him.

Surveillance and intelligence sharing between Canada and the United States increased significantly following the "9/11" attack, and in 2002 the RCMP shared information with US authorities about Mr. Maher Arar, a Canadian citizen who was born in Syria and had lived in Canada with his family since 1987. This information indicated that Arar was a "person of interest" in connection with its investigations of terrorism. During a stopover in New York as he was returning to Canada from a vacation in Tunisia, Arar was detained by US authorities who sought further information about him from the RCMP. They were informed that Arar was on a "watch list" and had links to the al-Qaeda terrorist organization. After receiving this information, the United States deported Arar to Syria, where he was imprisoned for more than a year. Arar subsequently claimed that he had been tortured while imprisoned in Syria (Canada, Commission of Inquiry 2006, 14).

After Arar was eventually released and returned to Canada, the Canadian government set up a commission of inquiry in 2004 to investigate the circumstances of his deportation to Syria and the role of the RCMP in this connection. In 2006 the Commission submitted its first report, in which it characterized the information that the RCMP had passed to US authorities as "inaccurate, portrayed him in an unfairly negative fashion, and overstated his importance in the RCMP investigation" (Canada, Commission of Inquiry 2006, 13), and that this information had likely contributed to the US decision to deport him to Syria. The Commission also concluded that "when briefing the Privy Council Office and senior government officials about the investigation regarding Mr. Arar, the RCMP omitted certain key facts that could have reflected adversely on the Force," and that both before and after Arar's return to Canada, the RCMP had "leaked confidential and sometimes inaccurate information about the case to the media for the purpose of damaging Mr. Arar's reputation or protecting their self-interests or government interests" (Canada, Commission of Inquiry 2006, 14, 16).

Following the release of the Commission's report, Commissioner Zaccardelli was summoned to appear before the House of Commons Standing Committee on Public Safety and National Security to explain the RCMP's role in the Arar affair, and in particular what he, as commissioner, had known about this, when he had known about it, and his communications with the Solicitor General of Canada (the minister responsible for the RCMP) about it. Zaccardelli appeared before the Committee in September 2006, ten days after the Commission's report had been published.

He told the Committee that he had become aware of the circumstances of Mr. Arar's deportation to Syria shortly after it occurred, and that the information that the RCMP had conveyed to US authorities about Arar had been incorrect. He said that the RCMP had informed US authorities that the information provided was not correct, and had kept the Solicitor General and his successor constantly briefed as the situation evolved.[3]

After he gave this evidence to the Committee, however, commentators began to point out that it did not square with the Commission's findings, or with the testimony that the Solicitor General and his successor had given in the Commission's hearings. Zaccardelli requested that he be given an opportunity to appear before the parliamentary committee again, to "clarify" his earlier evidence. In his second appearance, on December 5, 2006, he told the Committee that his earlier evidence had been mistaken, and that in fact he had not known the details of the RCMP's involvement in Mr. Arar's deportation to Syria until he had read about them in the Commission's report ten days before he had appeared before the Committee. From the Commission's report he had learned that "no senior staff—including myself—were told of the inaccuracies in the information provided to the Americans" in 2002. Explaining this extraordinary reversal of his earlier evidence to the Committee, he said:

In my testimony on September 28, I clearly inferred that some of the knowledge I got when I read the [Arar Commission] report. I implied that I may have had it in 2002. That was a mistake on my part, and that's why I wanted to come back here to correct the record. (Canada, House of Commons, Standing Committee on Public Safety and National Security, 2006, 7)

Zaccardelli insisted that he had not intentionally misled the Committee in his earlier evidence, and said:

> Mr. Chairman, I want to be very clear about the significance of what I have said here today. For a government official, nothing is more fundamental than ensuring that the information they provide to ministers is accurate and complete. To improperly withhold information or to misrepresent facts is a cardinal sin. If I had been guilty of such actions, no one would have to ask for my resignation. (Canada, House of Commons, Standing Committee on Public Safety and National Security, 2006, 5)

Committee members, however, insisted that he must resign. He submitted a letter of resignation to the Prime Minister on the following day, which was immediately accepted (Leblanc 2006).

India

Case One: Politics at the Top

T. R. Kakkar served as police commissioner for Delhi State, which includes the national capital of New Delhi, in 1997–98. On the second day of his appointment he was summoned to the home of the Indian Prime Minister (Kakkar 2005). After congratulations "in the true spirit of an Indian leader," the Prime Minister sympathized about the job the commissioner faced and hoped that he would hold to account any officers "guilty of excesses." He then expressed doubts about an investigation that the Delhi police had conducted into the kidnapping and murder of a Central Government Health Service doctor at Pandar Park. He "obliquely hinted" that individuals in the Delhi police were shielding the real culprit and that a "very important political leader" may have been involved. "I quickly saw the writing, in the direction in which

I was being pushed, and saw the hidden meaning behind the briefing" (p. 173). "It was a difficult situation. [The] 'Chief Executive' of the Country was giving me a story. In all fairness it should have been accepted by me as the total truth and acted upon" (p. 173). Kakkar replied, "sheepishly" he admits, that he knew nothing about the case but would examine the investigation himself and, if evidence of incompetence or malfeasance was found, he would reopen the investigation.

In little over a week, he reported his findings personally to the Prime Minister. He had found no evidence that the named politicians had a "hand in the disappearance of the doctor" (p. 174). The Prime Minister "looked at me hard," perhaps "looking at ways and means of taking me to the charted path in this particular case" (p. 174). Kakkar offered to send the case to the Lt. Governor of the State for forwarding to the Central Bureau of Investigation, the investigative arm of the Prime Minister's own government. "He did not give any reply to my suggestion and only said that I could go" (p. 175). Kakkar made no further inquiries and did not forward the case to the Lt. Governor.

This was by no means the end of Kakkar's difficulties with politicians. The Chief Minister, the top elected officer of Delhi State, gave him a list of people "almost every second night" that he wanted posted as commanders to Delhi's police stations or to the traffic police (p. 177). The Chief Minister felt, Kakkar said, that "like any others in the country he could also lord over the police and post officers and men as per his choice" (p. 177). Kakkar's response was to vet the list and remove any with "dubious records." He estimated that only 5 percent had clean records. Kakkar complained about this interference to the Lt. Governor and the central government's Home Minister. The Home Minister was always non-committal, once observing "Listen, do what is possible easily. What can I say about these issues?" (p. 179).

While standing firm against the Chief Minister's "daily" interference, Kakkar had a shrewd appreciation of the obligations of the minister:

A political leader who assembles his darbar [reception] every morning and pretends to be listening to the grievances of his constituents is in fact paying on lip service in most of the cases. Because, it is suicidal for him to say no to anyone who approaches him for favors. There, just to keep the flock together everyone practically is assured by the leader and his henchmen that his work would be done and that he can go back to sleep in peace. Which in fact is not the case. (p. 181)

Case Two: Politics in Criminal Investigations[4]

While serving as Superintendent of Police in Patna, the capital of the State of Bihar, Arvind Verma, a member of the nationally recruited Indian Police Service, was summoned to the office of the Chief Minister (1982). He was asked to explain why he was investigating the head of a local, private institute of aeronautical engineering. The Bihar government, according to the Chief Minister, was planning to grant corporate status to the enterprise, even though it had no facilities for flying and was operating out of the proprietor's small garden. Verma believed the proprietor should be prosecuted for fraud and return the students' money. The Chief Minister protested something to the effect, "Verma ji! There is no crime here." He did, however, agree to ask the proprietor to return the money. When the money was returned, the complainant withdrew his allegation of cheating, the Chief Minister dropped the plans to incorporate, and Verma did not pursue the investigation.

When Verma was Superintendent of Gaya District, he filed a case of extortion, nonpayment of wages, cheating, and forgery against some brick-kiln owners (1988). These small industries exploited tribal people by advancing them money and then working them ten to twelve hours a day for a pittance under very harsh conditions. Verma had been alerted to this practice by a local non-governmental organization. A Chief Minister again summoned him to the capital and asked him to stop the police action. When Verma protested, the Chief Minister abruptly ended the meeting and transferred the matter to the labor commissioner. A week later, Verma was transferred out of his district and sent to headquarters in the capital.

Verma recounts that political directions were sometimes transmitted through police officers further up the chain of command. This happened when a senior officer directed him not to take criminal action against a notorious son of a government minister. The officer ordered Verma to inform him of any wrongdoing by the son, so that he could speak to the minister about restraining his son. When Verma nonetheless filed charges against the son for murder and cheating, he was transferred to the Home Guards.

Throughout his tenure as a senior police officer, Verma frequently received petitions signed by the Chief Minister and other senior ministers to recruit a particular person to the police, withdraw criminal charges, or transfer a subordinate officer from his post.

Verma believes that politicians behaved more carefully when they knew an officer would act independently. In these cases, they would suggest or imply rather than issue direct orders.

New Zealand

Case One: Political Transition

Peter Doone was appointed as commissioner of the New Zealand Police in 1996, having previously served as deputy commissioner. He served as commissioner for just four years before resigning in 2000. His predecessor had signed a large contract for a new high-tech information and communications system (Integrated Crime Information and Communications System—INCIS) which had been pioneered in North America. As Deputy Commissioner, Doone had been given lead responsibility for overseeing implementation of the contract, and of course assumed final responsibility for this when he became commissioner. Implementation involved numerous problems, including significant cost overruns, and there was growing concern that it was not going to be successful. At the same time, Doone was facing increasing government demands for "efficiency savings," including budget cuts and demands for substantial staff reductions. The Police Association was complaining that delivery of basic services and equipment were being adversely affected. The INCIS contract was finally abandoned in 1999, at great taxpayer expense. The government set up a commission of inquiry to look into what had gone wrong.

In November 1999, the Labour Party, which in opposition had been highly critical of the National Party government and the New Zealand Police over their management of the INCIS contract, was elected to office. The new government, therefore, was already not well disposed toward Doone's performance as commissioner. Within a few weeks of the election, however, a story broke in the media according to which Doone and his female companion had been pulled over on election night as they were driving home from a party, apparently for driving after dark without lights on. The stop was made by a young constable who had only been on the job for three days. Doone's companion had been driving, but Doone had stepped out of the vehicle and had a conversation with the constable who, the story alleged, was carrying a "sniffer" and had indicated that he intended to ask the driver to take a breath test.[5] Evidence of what Doone said to the constable was never definitively established, but it evidently persuaded the constable not to pursue the matter further, and the constable later said that when he realized who the person he was speaking to was, he "felt nervous and overawed."

An investigation by the deputy commissioner into Doone's conduct on that occasion concluded that there was not sufficient evidence to charge Doone with obstruction of justice, a judgment agreed to by the Solicitor General who had been asked for a legal opinion on the matter. The deputy commissioner's report nevertheless concluded that Doone's conduct had been "inappropriate,"[6] and his report was forwarded to the Police Complaints Authority for review. In its report to the Attorney General, the PCA characterized Doone's conduct as "undesirable." The Attorney General gave Doone the opportunity to respond before she was to make a recommendation to the Cabinet as to whether Doone should continue in office. The day before the Cabinet was due to meet to discuss the matter, however, Doone tendered his resignation, which was accepted (Small, 2000).

Five years later Doone launched a defamation suit against the Prime Minister, alleging that she had "leaked" incorrect information about his conduct to the media at the time, which cast him in an unfavorable light and had led to further media stories that made it untenable for him to continue in office (Tunnah 2005). Doone had originally sued the newspaper that had published these stories, and only discovered that the Prime Minister had been the source when the newspaper revealed this in papers that it filed in its defense against the lawsuit. The Opposition and some media commentators interpreted the Prime Minister's passing of such information to the media as a ploy to force Doone to resign (Hide 2005; Wishart 2008, Chap. 2).

United States

Case One: Questionable Influence

During 2007–08 the Attorney General of New York State investigated two sets of charges of improper involvement of the Governor's office in activities of the New York State Police (Kaye 2010; Office of the Attorney General 2007). The Governor is the highest elected official in the state.

In the first case, the opposition majority leader in the New York Senate charged that the Governor had ordered the State Police to conduct an open-ended surveillance of his activities, in particular to produce records about the use of the State Police helicopter for public business.

In the second case, the New York State Police (NYSP) were charged with deferring inappropriately to political direction across the administrations of three Governors (one Republican, two Democratic) over approximately ten years. Specifically, the allegations were (New York Times 2010; Albany Times Union 2013):

- The NYSP "sanitized" the incident report of domestic violence involving a Republican member of the US House of Representatives.
- The Governor's NYSP protection detail and the Governor himself contacted a woman in New York City who placed an emergency call to the New York City police alleging an assault by a senior member of the Governor's staff.
- The Governor's office bypassed protocols in selecting the chief of the NYSP protection detail.
- The Governor's office misused the protection detail for personal errands, such as walking the Governor's dog and taking his children to social events.
- Aides to the Governor pressured an NYSP official to appoint a former campaign contributor to a uniformed post as deputy administrator despite having had no law-enforcement experience.
- Allowed the chief of the NYSP protection detail undue influence in determining promotions, allowed a Trooper to keep his badge after retirement, quashed the firing of a trooper who had been intoxicated on duty, and improperly investigated the Governor's campaign office and several prominent persons.

In both cases the investigations by the Attorney General's office found the specific allegations to be unfounded. However, when the second report was released, the Governor's Deputy Secretary for Public Safety resigned as did the Superintendent of the State Police. The report admonished the Governor and the State Police for failing to manage the appearance of undue influence and for errors of judgment in managing the Governor's protection detail.

The Governor's Office should set the standard for diligence in avoiding political interference with State Police business. The Superintendent of the State Police must conduct the business of the State Police in a wholly apolitical manner and *must avoid even the appearance of partisan activities within the State Police*. A new ethics policy should be promulgated establishing protocols between the Governor's Office and the State Police to this effect. (Emphasis added).

In response to the second investigation, the Attorney General wrote a letter to the Governor making six recommendations for the conduct of business between the State Police and the Governor's office:

- No political appointments to the NYSP uniformed ranks.
- A clear, direct line of communication between the NYSP Superintendent and the Secretary to the Governor.
- No acting appointments of Superintendents to the NYSP; vacancies in the post should be filled quickly.
- No "sanitizing" of investigation reports.
- The Secretary to the Governor should not be given protective services and driver unless justified by threat assessment.
- The Secretary to the Governor tasked with liaison to the NYSP should be a law enforcement professional.

Case Two: A Cautionary Tale of Small-Town Policing[7]

In April 1993, thirty-nine-year-old Mike Berkow became chief of the Coachella police department in southern California, a desert town east of Los Angeles. Two and a half years later, not quite at the end of his three-year contract, he resigned to become Police Chief in South Pasadena, California. In between, he and his officers arrested the Coachella mayor several times on charges of public drunkenness and domestic violence; worked with the county District Attorney to investigate the city manager for outstanding traffic warrants, failing to pay child support, and misuse of public funds; and successfully fended off efforts to reinstate the same city manager after his arrest for mismanagement of city funds.

Berkow had been hired by a strong, progressive city manager who, unfortunately for Berkow, was fired a short time later for resisting directions from the mayor and the city council. Two weeks after his appointment, Berkow approved the arrest of the mayor for public drunkenness and domestic violence against his wife at his illegally situated mobile home. There was a police video of him screaming at the arresting officers, ordering them to move away from the patrol car because as mayor he "owned it."

After the resignation of the city manager, Berkow was directed by the council to conduct a background check on the primary replacement candidate for the job—John Croswhite. Berkow initially refused because that would put him in the position of investigating a person who could become his boss. He eventually agreed, however, and later informed the city attorney that Croswhite had been fired for forgery from his previous job as development director in another city. Croswhite also consistently refused to provide requested documents to Berkow's background investigators. Berkow advised the city attorney, the mayor, and council against hiring Croswhite. The council, consisting of the mayor and four council members, hired him nonetheless, with the recommendation of the city attorney.

As might be expected, Berkow's relations with the council became very hostile, so much so that he ordered all police interactions with council members when the police were engaged in official business to be audio recorded and for videos to be made of meetings that became confrontational. In addition to arresting the mayor, he arrested a council member for building concealed compartments in automobiles, a felony in California, that he used for selling methamphetamine. At one time or another, the Coachella police arrested several members of another council member's family—father, mother, brother, nephews—on drug charges and other offenses. Curiously, however, this member never complained about the arrests.

City Manager Croswhite was a disaster. He held no staff meetings and failed to co-ordinate the work of the city's departments. At one point he refused to approve Berkow's proposal that all city employees have valid driver's licenses. Berkow then discovered that Croswhite himself not only did not have a valid license but had outstanding warrants against him for traffic offences.

The climax of Berkow's struggle with the City Manager came when he notified investigators from the Riverside County District Attorney's office about Croswhite's outstanding warrants and they arrested him. Berkow asked that the arrest be made shortly before a council meeting so that he could immediately provide details. The council suspended Croswhite without pay and appointed Berkow as acting city manager. Berkow then discovered that Croswhite had been working both as city manager and acting finance director. In these dual roles he had issued bonds without security and had run up huge charges on his own and the previous city manager's city-issued credit card.

After intense negotiations within the council, perhaps involving blackmail of one member by another, the council reversed itself within two weeks and voted three to two to re-hire Croswhite as interim city manager and development director if he would agree to plead down to having committed misdemeanors. This would make Croswhite once again Berkow's supervisor.

On the night of the vote to re-appoint Croswhite, the mayor learned about the fraudulent credit card charges and that Croswhite was likely to face additional criminal charges. The mayor then switched his vote and the council decided, by another three to two vote, against lifting the suspension. Croswhite was eventually convicted and forbidden from holding public office ever again.

Conclusion

These examples show that police governance can be seriously troubled in each country we have studied. The book will analyze these troubles comparatively, looking for patterns in the disputes and the factors which aggravate or mitigate their occurrence.

Notes

1.   See Loane (1996) and Dodkin (2003, 138) who claimed that Lauer resigned after the police minister had "pointedly suggested that he should consider his future."

2.   This was not the only concern the new government had with Overland's performance. As a result of a very public dispute between Overland and his deputy commissioner, the government had ordered an independent review of Victoria Police's senior command. Overland had apparently suspected that his Deputy had been the "whistleblower" who had triggered the Ombudsman's investigation.

3.   His successor's title had changed to Minister for Public and Emergency Preparedness. Zaccardelli's evidence to the Committee is reported in Canada, House of Commons, Standing Committee on Public Safety and National Security (2006).

4. This account was provided by Arvind Verma, now a professor at Indiana University, United States.
5. In his statement to the deputy commissioner's investigation into the incident, the constable concerned said that he had not intended, or asked, to administer a breath test, and that he wasn't sure whether the "sniffer" was in his hand or in his pocket (Wishart 2008, chap. 2).
6. His report can be accessed online at http://www.berenddeboer. net/politics/RobinsonReport.pdf.
7. This account was provided by former-chief Michael Berkow, supported by information provided in local newspapers.

References

Albany Times Union, 21-22 July 2013.

Brouwer, G. 2011. *Report: Investigation into an Allegation about Victoria Police Crime Statistics.* Melbourne, Vic.: Office of the Victorian Ombudsman. Retrieved from https://www.ombudsman.vic.gov. au/getattachment/c1b72649-5bfa-43ef-a7ed-9903328dd12f.

Canada, Commission of Inquiry into the Actions of Canadian Officials in Relation to Maher Arar. 2006. *Report of the Events Relating to Maher Arar: Analysis and Recommendations.* Ottawa, ON: Minister of Public Works and Government Services.

Canada, House of Commons, Standing Committee on Public Safety and National Security. December 5, 2006. Evidence. Number 024, 1st Session, 39th Parliament, p. 3. Retrieved from http://cmte. parl.gc.ca/cmte/CommitteePublication.aspx?SourceId=187550& Lang=1&PARLSES=391&JNT=0&COM=10804.

Dodkin, M. 2003. *Bob Carr: The Reluctant Leader.* Sydney, NSW: UNSW Press.

Duncan, G., NSW Parliament Joint Select Committee upon Police Administration. 1993. *The Circumstances Which Resulted in the Resignation of the Honourable E.P. Pickering, MLC, as Minister for Police and Emergency Services: First Report.* Sydney, NSW: NSW Parliament.

Edwards, R. October 3, 2008. "Met Police Chief Sir Ian Blair Forced Out by Mayor Boris Johnson." *The Telegraph.* Retrieved from http:// www.telegraph.co.uk/news/newstopics/ianblair/3124924/Met- police-chief-Sir-Ian-Blair-forced-out-by-mayor-Boris-Johnson.html.

Ferguson, J. March 6, 2013. "Ted Baillieu's Scandal Tapes Admission Fuels Leadership Turmoil." *The Australian.*

——. April 5, 2014. "ALP Puts Overland Rift in Election Focus." *The Australian.*

Hencke, D. November 6, 2006. "Met Chief Steps Back in Peerage Inquiry." *The Guardian.*

Hide, R. May 9, 2005. "Did the PM Treat Doone with Honesty and Integrity? Extract from a Press Conference." *Scoop.* Retrieved from http://www.scoop.co.nz/stories/PA0505/S00207/did-the-pm-treat-doone-with-honesty-and-integrity.htm.

Jones, N. January 3, 2014. Secret Support from Government Law Officers for South Yorkshire Police During Miners' Strike." *Nicholas Jones Archive and Blog.* Retrieved from http://www.nicholasjones.org.uk/articles/40-trade-union-reporting/277-secret-support-from-government-law-officers-for-south-yorkshire-police-during-miners-strike.

Kakkar, T. R. 2005. *Agony and Ecstasy.* New Delhi, India: Siddharth Publications.

Kaye, Judith S. 2010. *Report of the Investigation into the Response by the New York State Police and Others to a Domestic Incident Involving David W. Johnson, An Aide to the Governor.* Albany, NY: Office of the Attorney General of State of New York.

Laville, S. November 2, 2008. "For a Champion of Diversity, a Legacy of Little Change." *The Guardian,* p. 23.

Laville, S., and Dodd, V. October 4, 2008. "Johnson Defends Decision to Oust Met Chief." *The Guardian,* p. 9.

Laville, S., and Norton-Taylor, R. October 3, 2008. "Revealed: The Tory Plot that Forced Out Met Chief Blair." *The Guardian,* p. 1.

Leblanc, D. December 7, 2006. "Zaccardelli Takes the Fall." *The Globe and Mail,* p. A1.

Levy, M. June 16, 2011. "I wasn't pushed," says Overland of resignation." *The Age.* Melbourne, Vic.

Loane, S. January 16, 1996. "Exit the Unflappable Leader, Professional to the End." *Sydney Morning Herald.*

Moss, S. November 2, 2009. "Ian Blair: 'I Would Have Served Boris and Served Him Well.'" *The Guardian.*

Munro, P. May 8, 2011. "Call to Take Politics Out of Top Police Appointments." *The Age.* Melbourne, Vic.

New South Wales, Commission to Inquire into New South Wales Police Administration [Commissioner: Mr. Justice E. Lusher]. 1981. *Report*. Sydney: Government Printer.

New York Times, editorial, September 17, 2010.

Office of the Attorney General, State of New York. 2007. "Report of Investigation into the Alleged Misuse of New York State Aircraft and the Resources of the New York State Police." Albany, NY.

Porter, H. October 5, 2008. "He Should Have Stuck to Being a Policeman, not a Politician." *The Observer*, p. 31.

Reiner, R. 1991. *Chief Constables: Bobbies, Bosses or Bureaucrats?* Oxford: Oxford University Press.

Silverman, J. November 11, 2005. "'Political Police' Prompts Questions." *BBC News*. Retrieved from http://news.bbc.co.uk/2/hi/uk_news/4429716.stm.

Small, V. January 26, 2000. "Unrepentant Doone Forced to Step Down." *The New Zealand Herald*.

Stenning, P. 2008. "Brief Encounters: A Tale of Two Commissioners." In *Honouring Social Justice of Criminal Law: Essays in Honour of Dianne Martin*, edited by M. Beare, 328-48. Toronto, ON: University of Toronto Press.

Telegraph.co.uk. October 6, 2008. "Sir Ian Blair: The Resignation Statement in Full." *The Telegraph*. Retrieved from http://www.telegraph.co.uk/news/newstopics/ianblair/3123888/Sir-Ian-Blair-the-resignation-statement-in-full.html.

Tunnah, H. April 28, 2005. "PM to Fight Defamation Claim." *The New Zealand Herald*.

Wishart, I. 2008. *Absolute Power: The Helen Clark Years*. North Shore, NZ: Howling at the Moon Publishers.

3

History and Research

This chapter provides intellectual context for the research we have undertaken. It begins with a review of the history of relations between police and governments in Common Law jurisdictions. We then review some of the key literature on this relationship that has emerged in the six countries we have studied.

Police–Government Relations in Common Law Countries

Ever since the so-called "new police" were first established in London in 1829, there has been debate over the relationship between these modern police services and the governments under which they serve. In his history of the British police, Sir Charles Reith drew a distinction between "Ruler-appointed, Totalitarian Police" and "Kin-Police, or Democratic system" police (Reith 1952, 253). The distinction has been taken up by other writers and is commonly referred to as "regime policing" and "democratic policing" (Bayley 1985; Daruwala and Doube 2005). "Regime policing" refers to situations in which the police are expected to serve the interests of the particular rulers at the time. Their principal role is seen as maintaining the regime in power. This style of policing is particularly characteristic of colonial governments, with the police serving the interests of the foreign rulers rather than the colonized populace. That tradition has continued in some countries in their independent, postcolonial days. By contrast, "democratic policing" refers to police who serve the interests of the public at large rather than the exclusive interests of the government in power. This understanding of the role of the police has often come to be referred to as "policing by consent" or, more recently, "community-based" policing.

The regime/democratic distinction is helpful because it implies different relationships between governments and police. "Regime policing" implies a high degree of government control over the police, whereas "democratic policing" has come to imply some degree of independence for the police from government direction. Although the dichotomy is useful analytically, it is not quite so straightforward conceptually. In a liberal democracy the government is also supposed to reflect the public interest and to govern "by consent" rather than exclusively in the partisan interests of the political party or parties that happen to form the government at a particular time. Nor is the dichotomy so straightforward in practice. There is little consensus as to what degree of "police independence" is appropriate or acceptable in a democracy (Stenning 2007). Determining when government decisions reflect narrow partisan interests or some broader "public interest" is not always easy. Indeed, in the United States the term "police independence" is rarely used, and understandings of the police–government relationship have not been based on that concept.

The "new police" created by Sir Robert Peel in Britain are credited with the invention of "democratic policing." This is historically correct, but it overlooks a less consensual style of policing also associated with Britain. The British government had established police forces in Ireland at least fifty years before the establishment of the London Metropolitan Police in 1829 (Palmer 1988). Those police forces can reasonably be described as "regime" rather than "democratic" police. They became the model for police forces that were subsequently established in British colonies later in the nineteenth century—the Indian Police Service in 1861 (Dhillon 2005), the Armed Constabulary in New Zealand in 1867 (Hill 1989), the Northwest Mounted Police in Canada in 1873 (Chambers 1906/1973), and the State Police forces in Australia (Finnane 1994).

There have been suggestions that these early British colonial police forces were to some extent modeled on the earlier French Gendarmerie, a military-style police (Brodeur 2010, 75). It was this pedigree in fact that caused the English to have serious concerns about the establishment of Peel's "new police." Radzinowicz (1956) and others have chronicled the initial opposition that accompanied the establishment of these "new police," on the grounds that this institution would pose a threat to long-established British liberties. Similar concerns were raised about the introduction of plain-clothes detectives into Britain later in the nineteenth century, as they were thought to be French-style "government spies" (Emsley 2006).

Sir Robert Peel, as Home Secretary, was anxious to assuage these concerns when he created the "new" London Metropolitan Police. He adopted a number of strategies. First, he placed the police force under the governance of two "nonpolitical" commissioners who, he hoped, would be viewed as a buffer between the police and him. Second, he approved new "General Instructions" that emphasized that the police would be most effective if they developed close, respectful, and trusting relationships between themselves and the members of the communities they were policing. These are clearly stated as the fifth and seventh of the principles that are attributed to Peel—"Peel's Principles"—but were in fact developed by Charles Reith over a hundred years later (Lentz and Chaires 2007):

> The Fifth Principle. *To seek and preserve public favour, not by pandering to public opinion, but by constantly demonstrating* absolutely impartial service *to Law,* **in complete independence of policy,** *and without regard to the justice or injustice of individual laws; by ready offering of individual service and friendship to all members of the public without regard to their wealth or social standing; by ready exercise of courtesy and good humour; and by ready offering of individual sacrifice in protecting and preserving life.*

> The Seventh Principle. *To maintain at all times a relationship with the public that gives reality to the historic tradition that the police are the public and that the public are the police; the police being only members of the public who are paid to give full-time attention to duties which are incumbent on every citizen, in the interests of community welfare and existence.* (Reith 1952, 155–166, emphasis added)

In addressing the public's misgivings about the "new police," Peel argued that they were not really "new," but simply a more organized, efficient incarnation of the old police they replaced. He also emphasized that the police should have a measure of freedom from political or other external direction in the enforcement of the law. This strategy gave rise, especially during the twentieth century, to the doctrine of "police independence."

"Police independence" was modeled on a similar doctrine for the judiciary, which also emerged during the nineteenth century in Britain. It too stressed that the application of law should be enforced equally and impartially with respect to all citizens, regardless of any political or personal considerations. The notion of police independence, like that of judicial independence, can be regarded now as an essential element of the broader concept of "the rule of law," propounded particularly by the nineteenth century jurist Albert Dicey (1959).

The idea that police should have some legal immunity from government direction or "interference," especially with respect to their law enforcement activities, did not, however, take firm root in England or in Commonwealth countries until well into the twentieth century. Nineteenth century legislation establishing police services in countries like Canada, New Zealand, and Australia typically indicated that commissioners and chiefs of police were subject to the governance and direction of their police ministers, police boards, or commissions (Stenning 1982). In India, police are still regulated by the 1861 legislation created by the British colonial government (Chande 1997; Commonwealth Human Rights Initiative 2008; Daruwala, Joshi, and Tiwana 2005; Dhillon 2005; Verma 2000). Section 3 of the 1861 Act provides that:

> The superintendence of the police throughout a general police district shall vest in, and shall be exercised by, the State Government to which such district is subordinate; and except as authorised under the provisions of this Act, no person, officer or court shall be empowered by the State Government to supersede or control any police functionary. (*Police Act, 1861* [Act 5 of 1861])

The history of the police–government relationship has been very different in the United States. Despite the ostensible influence of the English approach, the tradition in the United States during the nineteenth century and well into the twentieth was of very direct political control and influence over police chiefs who were generally appointed by and acted under the supervision of elected city mayors and state governors (Fogelson 1977; Miller 1999; Monkkonen 1981; Robinson 1975). The idea of independence from political direction did not gain acceptance until the 1920s when some progressive police chiefs, such as August Vollmer in Berkeley, California, and his protegé, O.W. Wilson in Chicago, reacting to corrupt "Tammany Hall-style" practices, led a movement to "professionalize" the police, especially by challenging the hiring and promotion of police officers by "ward bosses" (Fosdick 1920; Jordan 1980; Sloat 2002; Smith 1960; Vollmer 1936; Walker 1977; Wilson 1950; Woods 1973). Although the tension between politicians and chiefs is widely acknowledged, in public discussions and writings it is not couched in terms of a required degree of "police independence."

In Britain there is considerable evidence that during the nineteenth and the early twentieth centuries the principle of police independence was reflected as much in its breach as in its observance. In his book, A History of Police in England and Wales (1967), Thomas Critchley provides numerous examples of circumstances in which police were specifically directed by their watch committees about how and against whom the law should be enforced.

Attitudes toward the relationship between police and central and local governments did not change substantially until the first half of the twentieth century when a number of authoritative statements about the relationship between police and governments lent support to the idea of police independence as a fundamental constitutional principle. In its 1929 report, the Royal Commission on Police Powers and Procedures commented that duties are imposed upon every constable by law and "cannot be widened or restricted by any superior officer or administrative authority" (Great Britain, Royal Commission on Police Powers and Procedure 1929, 15). However, at the same time it added remarks that seemed to qualify its support for police independence out of existence. It wrote that a chief constable was "responsible to his Police Authority" and should direct the activities of the force with their approval. It also stipulated that the chief constable was responsible to direct the activities of police officers to ensure that they properly discharge the duties of office.

A year later (1930), the decision of Mr. Justice McCardie in the case of *Fisher v. Oldham Corporation* gave a huge boost to the idea of police independence. Fisher claimed that he had been falsely arrested by members of the Oldham Police, and sued the Oldham Corporation, as the police's employer, for damages. In dismissing the case, Justice McCardie held, citing decisions in some earlier Australian cases, that for purposes of civil liability the relationship between the police and the Corporation could not be considered one of master and servant, because "If the local authorities are to be liable in such a case as this for the acts of the police with respect to felons and misdemeanours, then it would indeed be a serious matter and it would entitle them to demand that they ought to secure a full measure of control over the arrest and prosecution of all offenders" ([1930] 2 K.B. 364, at 372–373).

In 1962 the British Royal Commission on the Police invoked the judgment in the *Fisher Case* in support of its assertion that, with respect to what the Commission referred to as their "quasi-judicial" law enforcement functions of investigation, arrest, and prosecution in individual cases, "it is in the public interest that a Chief Constable . . . should be free from the conventional processes of democratic control and influence" (Great Britain, Royal Commission on the Police 1962, 30). Nevertheless, the Commission emphasized that this did not detract from the ultimate political accountability of the chief constable for such decisions. Remarking that "it appears odd that the constable enjoys a traditional status which implies a degree of independence belied by his subordinate rank in the force," the Commission argued that this "anomalous situation" is justified for the following reason:

> The constable, in carrying out many of the purposes we described at the beginning of this chapter, ought to be manifestly impartial and uninfluenced by external pressures. For much of the time he is not acting under orders and must rely on his own discretion and knowledge of the law. This consideration applies with particular force to police activities that are sometimes described as "quasi-judicial," such as inquiries in regard to suspected offences, the arrest of persons and the decision to prosecute. In matters of this kind it is clearly in the public interest that a police officer should be answerable only to his superiors in the force and, to the extent that a matter may come before them, to the courts. His impartiality would be jeopardised, and public confidence in it shaken, if in this field he were to be made the servant of too local a body. (Royal Commission on the Police 1962, 24)

Three years later, the Oxford political scientist Geoffrey Marshall published his seminal and influential book, *Police and Government* (1965), in which he disputed the doctrinal authenticity of the idea of police independence that the Commission had adopted. Arguing that this was not a sound basis for democratic police governance, he observed that "exaggerated and inconsistent as it is, [it] remains a hardy one and it has almost taken on the character of a new principle of the constitution whilst nobody was looking" (Marshall 1965, 120).

Marshall's reference to the "hardiness" of this doctrine was confirmed three years later by Lord Denning, the Master of the Rolls in England, in his judgment in the case of *R. v. Commissioner of Police, ex parte Blackburn* (1968). Blackburn, a Labour opposition member of the House of Commons, had initiated litigation to have the courts direct the commissioner of the Metropolitan Police to enforce the gambling laws against gaming clubs in London's Soho district. In the course of his judgment in the case, Lord Denning penned the following words which have since come to be regarded as the *locus classicus* of "police independence" in many Commonwealth countries around the world (Stenning 2007):

I have no hesitation, however, in holding that, like every constable in the land, [the Commissioner of the London Metropolitan Police] should be, and is, independent of the executive. He is not subject to the orders of the Secretary of State, save that under the Police Act 1964 the Secretary of State can call on him to give a report, or to retire in the interests of efficiency. I hold it to be the duty of the Commissioner of Police, as it is of every Chief Constable, to enforce the law of the land. He must take steps so to post his men that crimes may be detected; and that honest citizens may go about their affairs in peace. He must decide whether or not suspected persons are to be prosecuted; and, if need be, bring the prosecution or see that it is brought; but in all these things he is not the servant of anyone, save of the law itself. No Minister of the Crown can tell him that he must, or must not, keep observation on this place or that; or that he must, or must not, prosecute this man or that one. Nor can any Police Authority tell him so. The responsibility for law enforcement lies on him. He is answerable to the law and to the law alone. (R. v. Metropolitan Police Commissioner, ex parte Blackburn, [1968] 1 All E.R. 763, at 769)

Despite the withering criticism by Laurence Lustgarten in his book *The Governance of Police* (1986), this passage from Lord Denning's judgment is routinely referred to in government reports and white papers, reports of commissions of inquiry, memoirs of police chiefs, and academic treatises across the Commonwealth as encapsulating the proper relationship between police and government (Blair 2009; Canada, Commission of Inquiry 1981; Mark1978; Oliver 1987; Pitman 1998; Walker 2000; Whitrod 1976). Language in legislation implying greater authority for police ministers has been "read down" and interpreted to comply with Lord Denning's statement (see e.g., *R. v. Campbell* [1999] 1 S.C.R. 565 [Supreme Court of Canada]).

Major Academic and Government Literature

The considerable body of commentary on the police–government relationship that has been published since the Denning *dicta* in the Blackburn case has not been matched by empirical research. The first research of this kind was undertaken in Canada. In preparation for his 1975 book, *Police Command: Decisions and Discretion*, Brian Grosman, a lawyer without social science research training, interviewed a number of senior police officers about their responsibilities and relationships with politicians and police-governing authorities. The book made an important contribution by identifying key issues around police governance, accountability, and independence.

Another early starter in this vein was an exploratory study undertaken by Stenning in Canada, commissioned by the Federal Commission of Inquiry Concerning Certain Activities of the RCMP (Stenning 1981). The Commission considered whether to recommend the establishment of an independent commission or board to govern the Royal Canadian Mounted Police, which would act as a buffer between the force and the Solicitor General of Canada, who was the minister responsible for the RCMP. Stenning interviewed five categories of interviewees in each of the ten provinces of Canada: police commissioners and police chiefs, chairmen of provincial police commissions, chairmen of local police boards and commissions in the provincial capitals, presidents of police associations, and senior executives in provincial ministries responsible for policing. He reviewed the composition and mandates of provincial, regional, and municipal police boards and commissions in each province, and the legislation establishing them. Stenning found great variation on all of these matters among the provinces. Equally important, he found very little agreement among the interviewees about the limits of the respective mandates of police commissioners and chiefs, on the one hand, and police-governing authorities, on the other, with respect to the control and accountability of the police. Nor was there agreement on what the concept of "police independence" meant or implied. In particular, there was disagreement about the boundary between "policy" and "operational" policing decisions. These findings were confirmed by a similar but much bigger follow-up study of municipal and regional police services conducted across the country by the Canadian Police College in the early 1980s (Hann et al. 1985).

In England, police scholar Robert Reiner undertook a qualitative study involving interviews with almost all the chief constables in England and Wales. Although the relationship between police and government was not the central focus of his research, many of Reiner's interviewees commented on it. As indicated by the title of his book, *Chief Constables: Bobbies, Bosses or Bureaucrats?* (1991), Reiner identified different attitudes toward leadership among his interviewees, each of which generated different approaches to the relationship between chief constables, their local Police Authorities, and the Home Office, in the tripartite police governance arrangements that were in place in England and Wales at that time. Even though the doctrine of police independence that had been expounded by Lord Denning in the *Blackburn* case was by this time the received wisdom on this subject, Reiner found that its implications for the police–government relationship were interpreted quite differently by different chief constables.

Reiner identified four "ideal types" of chief constable, which he labeled the "Baron," the "Bobby," the "Boss," and the "Bureaucrat" (Reiner 1991, 306–309). Respectively, the Baron fears creeping politicization; the Bobby resents any attempt to influence his actions; the Boss resists in particular increasing control from the national government and any "left-leaning" undermining of the police; and the Bureaucrat believes that conflicts with politicians can be managed through "professionalism and diplomacy," and strongly favors robust local consultation.

More recently, Brian Caless, in *Policing at the Top: The Roles, Values and Attitudes of Chief Police Officers* (2011), reported that chief police officers viewed their relations with local and central governments as difficult and antagonistic. The chief police officers he interviewed had very little good to say about their Police Authorities, the central government's Inspectorate of Constabulary, or the Home Office. They also complained about what they regarded as political encroachment on their "operational independence" by overseers whom they regarded as ignorant, incompetent ("muddled amateurs"), and sometimes hostile. He quotes favorably the following comment by Adlam, a faculty member at the Police Staff College at Bramshill (Caless 2011, 171):

> The peculiar and 'sacred' doctrine of constabulary independence . . . seems to help sustain a generalized negative attitude towards the institutions and processes of government. So, for instance, Accelerated Promotion Course students admitted that they viewed central government either as an impediment, or a largely intrusive constraint, or an inconvenience 'around which they had to navigate'.

Caless reported that some of his interviewees thought fixed-term contract appointments for chief police officers, which are now the norm in England and Wales, encouraged improper interference by Police Authorities at renewal time. One interviewee said: "The PA [Police Authority] as a whole becomes more querulous, pickier, less satisfied, when it thinks it has you over a barrel" (Caless 2011, 61).

Unfortunately Caless did not explore the kinds of issues that most commonly generate police concerns about encroachments on operational independence. While a few of Caless' respondents seemed to be quite positive about their experiences in senior command positions, and some were optimistic about the future of policing, this was not true of the majority, most of whom came across as demoralized, pessimistic, and distrustful not only of the politicians to whom they were accountable, but also of the media, the public, and their peers.

In the early 2000s, the Australian Institute of Criminology commissioned a current police commissioner to interview serving and former colleagues in the Australian states. Although the police–government relationship was not the primary focus of these interviews, not surprisingly some of the interviewees commented on it. One said, "the role of commissioner has become much more public, more political" in recent years in Australia. Another said that "policing has become more political" and "the arms-length distance between politics and commissioners has shortened." And a third commented that there have been "direct and indirect attempts to control operational policing in an effort to please the media and the public, tightening the screws around the historical doctrine of the independence of the constable" (Dupont 2006, 90–91). Clearly, these commissioners felt that an historical tide was shifting against their independence.

In 2003, Dupont published an article in which he linked this transformation in the police–government relationship in Australia to the emergence of the "managerialism" of neoliberal "New Public Management," and in particular to the associated shift from "life tenure" to fixed-term contracts of employment for police commissioners:

> Aside from the fact that commissioners who want to pursue a career in policing will try to avoid at all costs a quarrel with their ministers, governments have also embedded in the former's contracts of employment very detailed performance clauses. Commissioner Ryan, in NSW, signed such an agreement, which covered police service operations, staff management and human resources, business administration and government priority areas. Each operational responsibility of the commissioner is therefore delineated in objectives and strategies to be implemented, which correspond to priorities determined by the government. When priorities change and when commissioners are not willing or able to accommodate these changes, the contractual arrangements permit a fast, if sometimes costly separation, as experienced by Commissioner Ryan in NSW in April 2002. In this context, the legal theory of the operational independence of the commissioner can no longer be sustained, as it is possible to discern a deliberate strategy from the political authorities to reassert their control over the police. (Dupont 2003, 22)

In 2004 Fleming undertook a review based on secondary sources of several instances of conflict between Australian police commissioners and police ministers from 1970 to 2004. She concluded that "the boundaries of the responsibilities and role of Police Commissioners and Police Ministers are not amenable to definition," and that "There can be no definitive legal statement of [a] Police Commissioner's and a Police Minister's role and responsibilities" (Fleming 2004, 70). In support of her observation, she cited Pitman's assertion (1998, 234) that "legislating roles and functions in itself does not reduce tensions between Police Ministers and commissioners." She suggested that the debate over the scope of proper political direction of the police should be set aside in favor of an approach based on "consultation and discussion" reflecting a relationship of "interdependence," rather than "independence":

> The interaction approach stresses mutual learning and co-operation. Management by negotiation replaces hierarchy. Much network activity is informal but it can have formal support. Joint meetings, seminars, away days, a shared secretariat are all common devices for promoting exchange. . . . The trick is to sit where the other person is sitting to understand their objectives and to build and keep trust between actors. (Fleming 2004, 71)

A similar approach to this issue was taken in the 1999 report of the Independent Commission on Policing for Northern Ireland (Patten Report), which recommended that the concept of police "independence" should be abandoned in favor of a concept of "operational responsibility," which it explained in the following terms:

> 6.21 Operational responsibility means that it is the Chief Constable's right and duty to take operational decisions, and that neither the government nor the Policing Board should have the right to direct the Chief Constable as to how to conduct an operation. It does not mean, however, that the Chief Constable's conduct of an operational matter should be exempted from inquiry or review after the event by anyone. That should never be the case. But the term "operational independence" suggests that it might

be, and invocation of the concept by a recalcitrant Chief Constable could have the effect that it was. It is important to be clear that a Chief Constable, like any other public official, must be both free to exercise his or her responsibilities but also capable of being held to account afterwards for the manner in which he/she exercises them. *We recommend that the Chief Constable should be deemed to have operational responsibility for the exercise of his or her functions and the activities of the police officers and civilian staff under his or her direction and control.* Neither the Policing Board nor the Secretary of State (or Northern Ireland Executive) should have the power to direct the Chief Constable as to how to exercise those functions. (UK, Independent Commission on Policing for Northern Ireland 1999, 32-33—emphasis in the original)

Despite changes in terminology, this approach does not appear to be significantly different from the approach recommended by the Royal Commission on the Police in 1962. It does, however, constitute a rejection of the much broader understanding of "police independence" advocated by Lord Denning in the *Blackburn* case in that it explicitly rejects the implication in the much-quoted passage that, with respect to their "law enforcement" functions, the police are not only immune from political direction and control but from political accountability too.

Despite the Patten Inquiry's attempt to re-formulate the police–government relationship in its report, a review of police governance arrangements in England and Wales by Her Majesty's Inspector of Constabulary ten years later concluded that:

Whilst the concept of operational independence has been widely accepted, the definition of it has remained so broad it provides limited practical guidance. The concept is, by its nature, fluid and context driven. As a result it is sometimes arguable where the governance responsibilities of police authorities end and the operational responsibilities of the chief constable begin. During our inspection work we found examples of how ambiguity as to "who is in charge" at different stages in making decisions can play out in day-to-day working between forces and authorities. (UK, HMIC 2010, 17)

There have also been several official inquiries, mostly in Australia and Canada, that have addressed particular situations in which this relationship has broken down, leading either to the resignation or dismissal of a commissioner of police or, less commonly, to the resignation of a police minister. Two such reports arose between police commissioners and the Labour Government in the Australian state of South Australia in the 1970s—the "Bright Report" (South Australia, Royal Commission 1971) and the "Mitchell Report" (South Australia, Royal Commission 1978). Similarly, the "Fitzgerald Report" and a Criminal Justice Commission report in Queensland both examined the breakdown of relations between Queensland police commissioners and the state governments of the day (Queensland, Commission of Inquiry1989; Queensland, Criminal Justice Commission 1992). The first led to the resignation of the state police commissioner, the second to the resignation of the police minister. These and similar situations generated a number of books and articles written by academics (Finnane 1990, 1994; Fox 1979; Manison 1995; Pitman 1998; Plehwe and Wettenhall 1979; Wettenhall 1977) and journalists (Cockburn 1979), as well as memoirs and biographies of key participants (Dunstan 1981; Whitrod 1976, 2001; Williams 2002).

In Canada, the role of the RCMP commissioner in the "Arar Affair" was the subject of extensive parliamentary scrutiny. In Australia and New Zealand, tensions between police commissioners and their governments, and allegations of improper political interference in policing, have also been the subject of parliamentary inquiries and reports (Duncan 1993a, 1993b; New Zealand, House of Representatives, 2000), and consultation documents prepared for them (Chen and Palmer 1998).

In United States the public, scholars, and the police themselves are certainly aware of the tension in governance between the police and politicians. No one is surprised by politicians who want to use the police for their own benefit. But they are unsure about what to do about it. As a result, instances of interference or lack of accountability are more likely to be met with shrugs than reform. This may explain why detailed, factual examination of the police–political relationship has attracted very little research from academics. The leading books, such as Walker's *The New World of Police Accountability* (2005), a second edition of which, co-authored by Carol Archbold, was published in 2014, focuses on the evolution of practices that can increase police accountability, not on the conduct of chiefs and politicians in "balancing" their responsibilities. Indeed, the term "police independence" is not mentioned in either of these books.

There have been three efforts to describe the perspectives of US chiefs based on interviews (Das and Marenin 2009; Isenberg 2010; Marenin and Das 2011; Tunnel and Gaines 1992). Only Tunnel and Gaines, however, get into the give-and-take of police governance. They concluded:

> The data indicate that Kentucky police chiefs must cope with varying levels of political pressures and interference, some legitimate and some illegitimate. Our study, for the most part, agrees with earlier findings. We found that political pressures are exerted from a variety of directions, and as a result, over 50 percent of the police chiefs in our

study who had left their jobs were forced out by governmental politicians . . . We have no measure as to how many
of these removals were justified . . . At this point, police
administration, at least in Kentucky, is severely bounded by
these relationships, which removes a large degree of management discretion from police administrators. (Tunnell
and Gaines 1992, 14–15)

Because their research was confined to only one US state
and was undertaken twenty-five years ago, it cannot be taken
as representative of the situation throughout the country
today, although its conclusions would still hardly surprise,
still less shock, Americans.

Accounts of the give-and-take between politicians and
chiefs are rare in the memoirs of either politicians or
police chiefs in the United States. Moreover, autobiogra-
phies by chiefs are themselves rare (Bouza 1990; Bratton
1998; Brown 2013; Gates 1992; Giuliani 2003; Murphy
and Plate 1977).

Finally, turning to India, it is not an exaggeration to say
that few people doubt that contemporary politicians interfere
with the decisions of police hiring, promoting, transferring,
disciplining, arresting, and investigating. And that they do so
at all command levels from police stations through districts,
regions, states, and the national government. The media write
about it constantly, often voicing public complaints about it
by senior police officers.

Public characterizations of the politicization of the police
by authoritative people are commonplace. For example, R. K.
Raghavan (2013), the former Director of the Central Bureau
of Investigation, said:

Under the present dispensation, the political executive has
a vice-like grip over the police and dictates how the latter
will and will not act.

. . . police investigations are prone to be dishonest and riddled with corruption. When the Executive has enormous discretion to interfere with investigations for serving political ends, regular police investigators enjoy equal discretion to indulge in malpractice.

. . . in a majority of States shocking political interference and venality are the order of the day.

This alleged cronyism is real and has become more and more blatant in spite of an intense media scrutiny of the political scene and public agencies like the police . . .

In a published interview, Kiran Bedi, the first female and perhaps best known police officer, said (Das and Marenin 2009, 133, 137):

Indeed, the political influence over the police has increased to an unprecedented extent and is badly affecting their performance.

Unfortunately, the police leadership has succumbed to political dictates and has become completely malleable.

Despite the frequency of public commentary, there are hardly any detailed case studies of political interference written by police officers, politicians, academics, or other observers. Indian police officers talk about interference freely off the record, but few write about it in detail, not even in memoirs after retirement. The shining exceptions to this are academic scholars Beatrice Jauragui at the University of Toronto, who has done extensive fieldwork with the Indian police, and Arvind Verma at Indiana University, who is a former senior police officer (IPS) (Jauregui 2013, 2014; Verma 2011). It is instructive that among people who write in English about

Indian police governance, those in India rarely provide case studies while those abroad do. The reason is self-censorship due to the fear of personal retaliation from politicians, as well as India's failure to develop a vibrant academic research infrastructure. It is certainly not systematic repression in public forums. India remains a vibrantly open society in terms of speech, association, and the media.

Conclusion

Since the creation of the "new police" in Britain in 1829, the relationship of the police to the governments under which they serve has been the subject of debate and controversy in all common law countries. In particular, how should they be held accountable for what they do? In the six countries we studied, concerns have been expressed about the possibility that the police will be deployed to serve the partisan interests of the governing party rather than the broader "public interest" of the citizenry at large. In only four of those countries (Australia, New Zealand, Canada, Britain), however, have serious efforts been made to establish rules or conventions designed to prevent this from happening by identifying some aspects of police work with respect to which the police should be recognized as requiring a measure of political independence from government direction. The scope of this independence has expanded and contracted as attitudes toward the need for oversight have changed, along with views about the appropriate institutions to manage the relationship. This chapter has reviewed the history of this concept and some of the most significant published academic and practitioner comment on it, recognizing that what is accepted as orthodoxy at one time may be viewed quite differently later. It also shows that the six countries have varied considerably in the attention they have devoted to the governance issue and the mechanisms they have chosen to regulate it.

References

Bayley, David H. 1985. *Patterns of Policing: A Comparative International Analysis.* New Brunswick, NJ: Rutgers University Press.

Blair, I. 2009. *Policing Controversy.* London: Profile Books.

Bouza, A. V. 1990. *The Police Mystique: An Insider's Look at Cops, Crime, and the Criminal Justice System.* New York: Plenum Press.

Bratton, W. J., with Knobler, P. 1998. *Turnaround: How America's Top Cop Reversed the Crime Epidemic.* New York: Random House.

Brodeur, J. P. 2010. *The Policing Web.* Oxford/New York: Oxford University Press.

Brown, L. P. 2013. *Growing Up to be Mayor: The True Story of Mayor Lee Brown, First African American Mayor of Houston.* Houston, TX: BGI Press.

Caless, B. 2011. *Policing at the Top: The Roles, Values and Attitudes of Chief Police Officers.* Bristol: The Policy Press.

Canada, Commission of Inquiry Concerning Certain Activities of the R.C.M.P. 1981. *Freedom and Security Under the Law: Second Report.* Ottawa: Minister of Supply & Services Canada.

Chambers, E. 1906. *The Royal North-west Mounted Police: A Corps history.* Montreal-Ottawa: The Mortimer Press. Reprint 1973 Toronto: Coles Publishing Co.

Chande, M. 1997. *The Police in India.* New Delhi: Atlantic Publishers & Distributors.

Chen & Palmer. 1998. *Constitutional Issues Involving the Police: An Analysis for the Independent External Review of the Police Administrative and Management Levels and Structures.* Wellington: Chen & Palmer.

Cockburn, S. 1979. *The Salisbury Affair.* Melbourne, Vic.: Sun Books.

Commonwealth Human Rights Initiative. 2008. *Police Organization in India.* New Delhi: C.H.R.I. Retrieved from http://www.humanrightsinitiative.org/publications/police/police_organisation_in_india_english.pdf.

Critchley, T. 1967. *A History of Police in England and Wales.* London: Constable.

Daruwala, M., and Doube, C. 2005. *Police Accountability: Too Important to Neglect, Too Urgent to Delay.* New Delhi: Commonwealth Human Rights Initiative. Retrieved from http://www.humanrightsinitiative.org/publications/chogm/chogm_2005/chogm_2005_full_report.pdf.

Daruwala, M., Joshi, G., and Tiwana, M. 2005. *Police Act, 1861: Why We Need to Replace It?* New Delhi: Commonwealth Human Rights Initiative.

Das, D. K., and Marenin, O. 2009. *Trends in Policing: Interviews with Police Leaders Across the Globe.* Boca Raton, FL: CRC Press.

Dhillon, K. 2005. *Police and Politics in India: Colonial Concepts, Democratic Compulsions: Indian Police 1947–2002.* New Delhi: Manohar Publishers.

Dicey, A. 1959. *Introduction to the Study of the Law of the Constitution.* 10th ed. London: Macmillan.

Duncan, G., NSW Parliament Joint Select Committee upon Police Administration. 1993a. *The Circumstances which Resulted in the Resignation of the Honourable E.P. Pickering, MLC, as Minister for Police and Emergency Services: First Report.* Sydney: NSW Parliament.

——. 1993b. *Remaining Issues: Final Report.* Sydney: NSW Parliament.

Dunstan, D. 1981. *Felicia: the Political Memoirs of Don Dunstan.* Crow's Nest, Vic.: Macmillan.

Dupont, B. 2003. "The New Face of Police Governance in Australia." *Journal of Australian Studies* 27 (78): 5–24.

——. 2006. "Power Struggles in the Field of Security: Implications for Democratic Transformation." In *Democracy, Society and the Governance of Security*, edited by J. Wood and B. Dupont, 86–110. Cambridge: Cambridge University Press.

Emsley, C. 2006. "From Ex-con to Expert: The Police Detective in Nineteenth Century France." In *Police Detectives in History 1750–1950*, edited by C. Emsley and H. Shpayer-Makov, 61–78. Aldershot: Ashgate.

Finnane, M. 1990. "Police and Politics in Australia—The Case for Historical Revision." *Australian and New Zealand Journal of Criminology* 23:218–28.

——. 1994. *Police and Government: Histories of Policing in Australia.* Melbourne, Vic.: Oxford University Press.

Fleming, J. 2004. "Les Liaisons Dangereuses: Relations Between Police Commissioners and Their Political Masters." *Australian Journal of Public Administration* 63 (3): 60–74.

Fogelson, R. 1977. *Big-city Police.* Cambridge, MA: Harvard University Press.

Fosdick, R. 1920. *American Police Systems.* New York: The Century Company.

Fox, R. 1979. "The Salisbury Affair: Special Branches, Security and Subversion." *Monash University Law Review* 5 (4): 251–70.

Gates, D, F., with Diane K. Shah, 1992. *Chief: My Life in the LAPD.* New York: Bantam Books.

Giuliani, R. 2003. *Leadership.* New York: Thorndike Press.

Great Britain, Royal Commission on the Police. 1962. *Final Report.* Cmnd. 1728. London: H.M.S.O.

Great Britain, Royal Commission on Police Powers and Procedures. 1929. *Report Cmnd. 3297.* London: H.M.S.O.

Grosman, B. 1975. *Police Command: Decisions and Discretion.* Toronto, ON: Macmillan.

Hann, R., McGinnis, J., Stenning, P., and Farson, S. 1985. "Municipal Police Governance and Accountability in Canada: An Empirical Study." *Canadian Police College Journal* 9 (1): 1–85.

Hill, R. 1989. *The History of Policing in New Zealand, Volume 2, The Colonial Frontier Tamed: New Zealand Policing in Transition, 1867–1886.* Wellington: Historical Branch, NZ Department of Internal Affairs/GP Books.

Isenberg, Jim. 2010. *Police Leadership in a Democracy: Conversations with America's Police Chiefs.* Boca Raton, FL: CRC Press.

Jauregui, Beatrice. 2013. "Beatings, Beacons, and Big Men: Police Disempowerment and Delegitimation in India." *Law and Social Inquiry* 38 (3): 643–69.

———, 2014. "Police and Legal Patronage in Northern India." In *Patronage as Politics in South Asia* (chapter 10), edited by A. Piliavsky. New York: Cambridge University Press.

Jordan, L. 1980. "Police and Politics: Charleston in the Gilded Age, 1880–1900." *The South Carolina Historical Magazine* 81 (1): 35-50. Retrieved from http://www.jstor.org/discover/10.2307/27567600?uid=3737536&uid=2129&uid=2&uid=70&uid=4&sid=21104528549203.

Lentz, S., and Chaires, R. 2007. "The Invention of Peel's Principles: A Study of Policing 'Textbook' History." *Journal of Criminal Justice* 35:69–79.

Lustgarten, L. 1986. *The Governance of Police.* London: Sweet & Maxwell.

Manison, G. 1995. "Managing Australia's Police: The Challenge to Identify Who Should be in Charge—Politicians or Police?" *Australian Journal of Public Administration* 54 (4): 494–506.

Marenin, O., and Das, D. K. (Eds.). 2011. *Trends in Policing: Interviews with Police Leaders Across the Globe.* Boca Raton, FL: CRC Press.

Mark, R. 1978. *In the Office of Constable–An Autobiography.* London: Collins.

Marshall, G. 1965. *Police and Government: The Status and Accountability of the English Constable.* London: Methuen & Co.

Miller, W. 1999. *Cops and Bobbies: Police Authority in New York and London, 1830-1870.* Columbus: Ohio State University Press.

Monkkonen, E. 1981. *Police in Urban America, 1860–1920.* Cambridge: Cambridge University Press.

Murphy, P. V., and Plate, T. 1977. *Commissioner: A view from the Top of American Law Enforcement.* New York: Simon and Schuster.

New Zealand, House of Representatives, Justice & Electoral Committee. 2000. "Inquiry into Matters Relating to the Visit of the President of China to New Zealand in 1999: Report of the Justice and Electoral Committee." Retrieved from http://www.gp.co.nz/wooc/i-papers/i7Aa-china.html.

Oliver, I. 1987. *Police, Government and Accountability.* London: Macmillan.

Palmer, S. 1988. *Police and Protest in England and Ireland 1780–1850.* Cambridge/New York: Cambridge University Press.

Patten Report, 1999. Independent Commission on Policing in Northern Ireland. *A New Beginning: Policing in Northern Ireland.*

Pitman, G. 1998. "Police Minister and Commissioner Relationships." Doctoral dissertation, Faculty of Commerce and Administration, Griffith University, Queensland, Australia.

Plehwe, R. 1973. "Some Aspects of the Constitutional Status of Australian Police Forces." *Australian Journal of Public Administration* 32 (3): 268–85.

Plehwe, R., and Wettenhall, R. 1979. "Reflections on the Salisbury Affair: Police-government Relations in Australia." *Australian Quarterly* 51 (1): 75–91.

Queensland, Commission of Inquiry into Possible Illegal Activities and Associated Police Misconduct (Fitzgerald Inquiry). 1989. *Report.* Brisbane, Qld: Government Printer.

Queensland, Criminal Justice Commission. 1992. *Report on an Inquiry into Allegations Made by Terence Michael Mackenroth, MLA, the Former Minister of Police and Emergency Services, and Associated Matters.* Brisbane: Queensland Criminal Justice Commission.

Radzinowicz, L. 1956. A History of English Criminal Law and Its Administration from 1750, Vol. 3: The Reform of the Police. London: Stevens & Sons.

Raghavan, R. K. 2013. "Story of a Caged Parrot, Part 2." Indian Express, August 17, 2013.

Reiner, R. 1991. Chief Constables: Bobbies, Bosses or Bureaucrats? Oxford: Oxford University Press.

Reith, C. 1952. The Blind Eye of History: A Study of the Origins of the Present Police Era. London: Faber & Faber.

Robinson, C. 1975. "The Mayor and the Police—The Political Role of the Police in Society." In Police Forces in History, edited by G. Mosse, 277–315. London/Beverley Hills, CA: Sage.

Sloat, W. 2002. A Battle for the Soul of New York: Tammany Hall, Police Corruption, Vice, and Reverend Charles Parkhurst's Crusade Against Them, 1892–1895. New York: Cooper Square Press.

Smith, B. 1960. Police Systems in America. 2nd ed. New York: Harper & Bros.

South Australia, Royal Commission. 1978. Report on the Dismissal of Harold Hubert Salisbury [The Mitchell Report, Commissioner: Madam Justice R. Mitchell]. Adelaide, SA: Government Printer.

South Australia, Royal Commission on the September Moratorium Demonstration. 1971. Report [The Bright Report, Commissioner: Mr. Justice Bright]. Adelaide, SA: Government Printer.

Stenning, P. 1981. Police Commissions and Boards in Canada. Toronto, ON: Centre of Criminology, University of Toronto.

——. 1982. Legal Status of the Police. Ottawa, ON: Law Reform Commission of Canada.

——. 2007. "The Idea of the Political 'Independence' of the Police: International Interpretations and Experiences." In Police and Government Relations: Who's Calling the Shots?, edited by M. Beare and T. Murray, 183-256. Toronto, ON: University of Toronto Press.

Tunnell, K., and Gaines, L. 1992. "Political Pressures and Influences on Police Executives: A Descriptive Analysis." American Journal of Police 11 (1): 1–16.

United Kingdom, Her Majesty's Inspector of Constabulary. 2010. Police Governance in Austerity: HMIC Thematic Report into the Effectiveness of Police Governance. London: H.M.I.C.

United Kingdom, Independent Commission on Policing for Northern Ireland (Rt. Hon. C. Patten, Chair). 1999. *Report–A New Beginning: Policing in Northern Ireland.* London: Crown copyright.

Verma, A. 2000. "Politicisation of the Police in India: Where Lies the Blame?" *Indian Police Journal* 47 (4): 19–37.

——. 2011. *The New Khaki: The Evolving Nature of Police in India.* Boca Raton, FL: CRC Press.

Vollmer, A. 1936/1971. *The Police and Modern Society: Plain Talk Based on Practical Experience.* Reprint. Montclair, NJ: Patterson Smith, 1971.

Walker, N. 2000. *Policing in a Changing Constitutional Order.* London: Sweet & Maxwell.

Walker, S. 1977. *A Critical History of Police Reform: The Emergence of Professionalism.* Lexington, MA: Lexington Books.

——. 2005. *The New World of Police Accountability.* Thousand Oaks, CA: Sage.

Walker, S., and Archbold, C. 2014. *The New World of Police Accountability.* 2nd ed. Thousand Oaks, CA: Sage.

Wettenhall, R. 1977. "Government and the Police" *Current Affairs Bulletin* 53 (10): 12–23.

Whitrod, R. 1976. "The Accountability of Police Forces–Who Polices the Police?" *Australian and New Zealand Journal of Criminology* 9: 7–24.

Whitrod, R. 2001. *Before I Sleep: Memoirs of a Modern Police Commissioner.* St. Lucia, Qld: Queensland University Press.

Williams, S. 2002. *Peter Ryan: The Inside Story.* Sydney: Viking/Penguin.

Wilson, O. 1950. *Police Administration.* New York: McGraw-Hill.

Woods, J. 1973. "The Progressives and the Police: Urban Reform and the Professionalization of the Los Angeles Police." Doctoral diss., University of California.

4

Settings and Systems

The research in this book is based on the premise that the practice and institutions of police governance vary across our chosen sample of countries. Because the countries are genuine democracies, there is an opportunity to compare experiences and possibly learn from them. This chapter describes those respective institutions of police governance. It also describes the larger governmental systems of which the police are a part as well as distinctive historical and contextual features.

Because the differences in governance and context are considerable, readers may find this chapter useful to refer to as we move from country to country in our analysis. We will explore these differences in three sections:

1. Geography, people, and crime
2. National systems of government
3. Institutions of police governance

At the end, we will discuss whether the variation in contexts is so great that it undermines the validity of comparison.

Geography, People, and Crime

The countries in our sample vary enormously in size and population. These differences are shown in Table 4.1, listing the countries in descending order of magnitude.

The countries obviously differ enormously in population. The population of India is 270 times that of New Zealand; Britain's is almost treble that of Australia. The US population is one-third that of India, but ten times larger than the next most populous country. In terms of geographical size, Australia, Canada, and the United States are two to three times the size of India. Britain, which looms so large in the history of all the other countries, is about the size of the US states of Michigan or Oregon. New Zealand is the size of Colorado.

These differences have important implications for the scale of police departments, and hence for the scale of police governance. Simply put, police governance is organized on radically different scales across our sample. The United States, for example, with the second largest land area, has approximately seventeen thousand independent police departments. Australia, with a land area 80 percent as large as the United States', has only eight. Britain has forty-three police services in an area the equivalent of a midsized US state. Britain, in effect, has many more police jurisdictions than much larger Australia or New Zealand, but many fewer than the United States. Because the Indian constitution assigns police authority to its states, it has thirty-two independent police agencies in an area equivalent to the land area of the United States east of the Mississippi. The scale of India's primary police agencies is more like US State Police agencies than its city or county agencies.

Canada, with the largest land area, has either approximately 179 or 340 police services depending on what is counted as a separate police service. According to Statistics Canada there are 178 general police services accountable

Table 4.1

	Population	Geographic Area (square miles)		Density	
India	1,184,639,000	Canada	3,851,807	India	933.27
United States	309,975,000	United States	3,717,811	Britain	960.9
Britain	56,100,000	Australia	2,967,908	United States	83.38
Canada	34,207,000	India	1,269,345	New Zealand	42.26
Australia	23,480,970	New Zealand	103,737	Canada	8.88
New Zealand	4,383,600	Britain	58,383	Australia	7.55

World Atlas, "Countries of the World," estimated 2012–14 (www.worldatlas.com).

exclusively to local political authorities (Burczycka 2013). In addition to its national policing responsibilities, however, the RCMP provides police services to 161 jurisdictions on contract to provincial and local authorities, including 8 provinces, 3 territories, and 150 municipalities. Under the terms of these contracts, provincial, territorial, and municipal authorities have some involvement in police governance. Thus, for the RCMP on-contract accountability is multiple, local, provincial, and national.

Police agencies customarily report the number of people whose safety they are responsible for. This is misleading because it does not account for the size of the area covered. Surely the problems of crime prevention and control are different with a population of one hundred people in one square mile than one hundred people in one-hundred square miles. In our sample, British police preside over jurisdictions with an average population of 1.3 million; US jurisdictions with an average of 18,000. The contrast between US and Indian jurisdictions is even more dramatic. India's population is three times larger than that of the United States, but occupies an area only 40% as large. So its 32 jurisdictions are responsible for an average of 348 million compared with United States' 18,000. There are similar differences in policing responsibilities between India and Australia/Canada. The differences are reduced to some extent by the fact that Australia's population is clustered in large cities along its coast, while Canada's is concentrated in cities along the border with the United States. Nonetheless, these figures indicate that the conditions of policing vary significantly within our sample. The problems of police governance, one can assume, would differ, as they would between New York City and rural Arizona or Sydney and outback South Australia.

Finally, all of our countries are diverse socially to varying degrees. English is an official language in all of them, although not exclusively in any except Australia. In the United

States, English is supplemented by Spanish in some states; in New Zealand by Māori; in Canada by French; in Britain by Welsh; and in India by 15 regional languages.

With respect to ethnic and cultural diversity, James Fearon constructed a "fractionalization" index for approximately 160 countries in 2003 (Fearon 2003). For our sample, he found that India was far and away the most diverse, followed by Canada, New Zealand, United States, Britain, and Australia.

With respect to crime, international comparisons are extremely unreliable. Indeed, there is considerable doubt about the reliability of data on many categories of crime within countries. Existing data suggest that of our six countries, Britain and New Zealand have the highest overall crime rates, and India the lowest, with the United States, Canada and Australia closely clustered in between (van Dijk et al. 2007, 43; India, National Crime Records Bureau 2013, 22). [1] India is the only country in our sample that is experiencing organized violence against the government and its police.

National Systems of Government

In this section we will cover each country's colonial history, form of government, national structure, and constitutional status.

1. Colonial history

All except Britain were once colonies. They vary significantly as to how long they have been fully independent, ranging from the United States (1776) to India (1947). [2] Canada became an independent Dominion in 1867, Australia a Commonwealth in 1901, and New Zealand an independent Dominion in 1907. The chief importance of this is that they have all inherited Common Law legal systems, albeit adapted to local conditions over the years. From the point of view of police–government relations, many features of statute and

Common Law have continued to be shared over the ensuing years. For example, judicial decisions in England, Canada, and New Zealand concerning the idea of police "independence" were significantly influenced by earlier Australian judicial decisions. In this tradition the United States and India are outliers. The United States has been almost entirely unaffected by police governance developments in the other countries, while policing in India has been regulated by the Police Act of 1861 that reflects a colonial mentality imposed by the British.

2. Forms of government

Four of our six jurisdictions have "Westminster-style" systems of parliamentary government. India also has a Westminster-style parliamentary system, but is a presidential republic. The United States has a legislative–executive system of government at all levels.

3. National structures

Australia, Canada, India, and the United States are federations consisting of national governments and subordinate states/provinces. Britain and New Zealand are both unitary states with one national government. Local government is significant in Canada, Britain, and the United States, but not in Australia, India, and New Zealand outside of a few large cities.

4. Constitutional status

Australia, Canada, India, and the United States have formal written constitutions; Britain and New Zealand do not. In the United States and Canada, these contain a list of guaranteed rights—respectively, the Bill of Rights and the Charter of Rights and Freedoms. In the United States and Canada, therefore, domestic legislation is required to be compliant with constitutional standards. The other four countries do not have such domestic constitutional documents. Britain is in the unusual position of having a domestic Human Rights Act (1988) that incorporates the European Convention on Human Rights adopted in 1947. New Zealand and the State of Victoria in Australia have human rights legislation in the form of regular statutes against which other statutes must be interpreted and applied.

Institutions of Police Governance

Apart from the broad structural features just discussed, there are a number of more specific structural considerations which need to be taken into account in understanding police-government relationships in the six countries:

- Degree of centralization
- Legal authorization
- Explicit institutions of governance
- Terms of appointment of chiefs.

1. Degree of centralization

Are police organized locally, regionally, nationally, or in some combination of these? Our six countries vary significantly in this respect, and consequently in the number of police agencies accountable to elected governments.

- New Zealand—1
- Australia—8
- India—36
- Britain—43
- Canada—179/340
- United states—estimated 17,000

In the United States and Canada, police services have been established at all governmental levels—national, state/provincial, county/regional, and municipal. The Federal Bureau of Investigation and the Royal Canadian Mounted Police (RCMP) respectively are federally organized police services, and are governed by and accountable to federal authorities—respectively, the US Department of Justice and the Canadian Ministry of Public Safety and Emergency Preparedness. These two police services have nationwide jurisdiction.

In the United States oversight is most commonly the responsibility of elected municipal mayors and councils. Police chiefs of US counties, who are called Sheriffs, are directly elected. In Canada, most municipal and regional police chiefs are governed by police boards or commissions. Their composition varies from province to province, some with a majority of elected members, others with a majority of appointed ones. The extent of devolution of policing responsibility to lower levels of government is determined by provincial legislation. For example, the appointment of members of their governing police boards or commissions may be made by provincial governments. This gives provincial governments a significant role in the governance and accountability of these local police services. They may also set minimum standards for the appointment of police chiefs, have appellate roles with respect to disciplinary matters, and authority to hold inquiries and audits of police services.

In Britain, police organization has always been decentralized. There are currently 43 police services, all organized regionally with the exception of the London Metropolitan Police and the City of London Police, which together are responsible for policing the capital. The City of London Police is responsible for the square-mile financial district. The regional police services are headed by chief constables, while the "London Met" and the City of London Police are headed by commissioners.

In Australia police services are established only at the central, state, and territory levels. This is true in India too by and large, although in recent years authority to create and govern police has been devolved to nine of the largest cities.

Most police in both Australia and India are accountable to state governments. The situation for the police in the capital cities of Australia and India is more complicated because they are accountable to both national and local supervision. The police of the Australian Capital Territory are a business unit of the Australian Federal Police (AFP), established under a "Purchase Agreement" between the Commonwealth (federal) and ACT governments. Its commissioner is always a senior officer of the AFP. The New Delhi Police is one of a handful of federal territorial police services which are governed by the national Minister of Home Affairs.

Of the six countries included in our research, New Zealand is the only one with a single police force governed by the national government via its police minister. The police commissioner is thus exclusively accountable to the national government.

2. Legislative provision for police governance

The policing statutes in some of the Canadian provinces and Australian states, the Indian Police Act, and until very recently the Metropolitan Police Act in England have offered no clear guide to police chiefs and politicians as to what their respective roles in police governance are supposed to be. Section 5 of the Canadian RCMP Act, for instance, simply provides that "(1) The Governor in Council may appoint an officer, to be known as the commissioner of the Royal Canadian Mounted Police, who, under the direction of the minister, has the control and management of the Force and all matters connected therewith." There is no indication in the Act as to what "the direction of the minister" might legitimately encompass, or what is or is not included under the rubric of "the control and management of the Force."

By comparison, the English Police Act of 1964 established the tripartite police governance arrangements for England and Wales stipulating fairly specifically the respective roles and responsibilities of chief constables, local Police Authorities, and the Home Secretary.

In the United States, state legislation and local ordinances govern the relations between state/local chiefs and their respective governments. By and large, politicians appoint chiefs, often with locally elected council approval. It is common in the United States to distinguish "strong mayors" who have extensive executive authority and "weak mayors" who must defer to elected councils. In some municipalities, city managers, who are appointed by mayors, are given authority for appointing and supervising police chiefs. They provide an explicit buffer between politicians and the daily administration of municipal government. According to a somewhat dated survey, less than 5 percent of municipalities are administered by nonpartisan, elected commissions (US Advisory Commission on Intergovernmental Relations 1999). A more recent study says simply that there is "extensive variance in local discretionary powers" (Bowman and Kearney 2011).

In Australia the first legislation to specify the roles of a minister and a commissioner was the Australian Federal Police Force Act of 1979. "General policy" was the preserve of the minister; "general administration" and "control of operations" of the commissioner (section 13).

(1) Subject to this Act, the Commissioner has the general administration of, and the control of the operations of, the Australian Federal Police.

(2) The Minister may, after obtaining and considering the advice of the Commissioner and of the Secretary [the departmental head of the Police Department], give written directions to the Commissioner with respect to the general policy to be pursued in relation to the performance of the functions of the Australian Federal Police.

(3) The Commissioner shall comply with all directions given under this section.

In 1990, the Australian state of Queensland introduced legislation which spelled out in some detail the responsibilities of the police commissioner and specified circumstances under which the police minister could issue directions to the commissioner. The legislation was prompted by the Fitzgerald Inquiry (Queensland Commission of Inquiry 1989) into police and government corruption and inappropriate government "interference" in the governance of the police force. Under the new legislation the Minister was authorized to issue directions concerning:

(a) The overall administration, management, and superintendence of, or in the police service; and (b) policy and priorities to be pursued in performing the functions of the police service; and (c) the number and deployment of officers and staff members and the number and location of police establishments and police stations." (Police Service Administration Act 1990)

The commissioner was required to comply with, and keep a register of, all such directions given.

The most recent legislative provisions of this kind were included in the Victoria Police Act of 2013 under the explicit heading "Relationship with government." Section 10 provides that the minister may "from time to time, after consulting with the Chief Commissioner, give written directions to the Chief Commissioner in relation to the policy and priorities to be pursued in the performance of the functions of Victoria Police." The section provides, however, that such directions may not be given in relation to the "preservation of the peace and the protection of life and property in relation to any person or group of persons," in particular

(a) enforcement of the law in relation to any person or group of persons;

(b) the investigation or prosecution of offences in relation to any person or group of persons;

(c) decisions about individual members of Victoria Police personnel, including decisions in relation to discipline;

(d) the organizational structure of Victoria Police;

(e) the allocation or deployment of police officers or protective services officers to or at a particular location;

(f) training, education, and professional development programs within Victoria Police;

(g) the content of any internal grievance-resolution procedures.

Section 11 of the Act, however, is equally specific as to the obligation of the chief commissioner to provide information or reports to the minister, thus ensuring a high degree of political accountability.

The Victoria Police Act is not only the most specific of any such legislative provisions currently in effect, but also the most restrictive in terms of the matters where political direction is not permitted.

In 2008, New Zealand enacted police legislation which includes the following provisions under the heading "responsibilities and independence of the Commissioner" (Policing Act of 2008, Section 16):

1. The commissioner is responsible to the Minister for—

    (a) carrying out the functions and duties of the police; and

    (b) the general conduct of the police; and

    (c) the effective, efficient, and economical management of the police; and

    (d) tendering advice to the minister and other ministers of the Crown; and

    (e) giving effect to any lawful ministerial directions.

2. The commissioner is not responsible to, and must act independently of, any minister of the Crown (including any person acting on the instruction of a minister of the Crown) regarding—

(a) the maintenance of order in relation to any individual or group of individuals,
(b) the enforcement of the law in relation to any individual or group of individuals,
(c) the investigation and prosecution of offences, and
(d) decisions about individual Police employees.

3. Institutions of police governance

Explicit institutions to mediate the relations between politicians and chiefs exist in Australia, Canada, New Zealand, and the United Kingdom. There are none in India and only a few in the United States. By and large, US politicians and chiefs are left on their own, subject only to vague legal directions.

In Britain, the forty-one provincial police services, excluding the London Metropolitan Police and the City of London Police, were governed until 2012 through what came to be known as the "tripartite system" involving shared responsibilities between the chief constable, a local "Police Authority," and the Home Secretary, who is a minister in the central government in Westminster. The Police Authority consisted of a majority of locally elected and a minority of appointed "independent" members. Over time the respective responsibilities of each element of the tripartite governance structure changed considerably, with increased authority and influence being accorded to the Home Secretary, largely at the expense of the local Police Authority. Chief constables have necessarily interacted with both local and central political authorities.

In 2011 Police Authorities were abolished by an act of parliament and replaced by locally elected Police and Crime Commissioners in each police jurisdiction. The PCCs are advised and "scrutinized" by appointed Police and Crime Panels consisting of a majority of persons appointed by the local council, and a small minority co-opted by the panel itself. In effect, the public now directly selects the primary local supervisor of the police. This is somewhat like the US sheriff system, although the PCCs do not become chief police officers. At the same time, the central Home Secretary still maintains a directive, advisory, and co-ordinating role.

The governing arrangements for the London Metropolitan Police and the City of London Police have always been *sui generis*. When the Met was created in 1829, its two commissioners were responsible exclusively to the Home Secretary. This was justified by the fact that, in addition to being responsible for the policing of the metropolis, the Met had some national policing responsibilities, and the Home Secretary has always been the central government minister responsible for policing. The 1996 *Police Act*, however, provided for the establishment of a Metropolitan Police Authority consisting of a majority of locally elected politicians and a minority of appointed members. The authority to appoint the commissioner, however, remained with the Home Secretary. A further change was introduced by the legislation establishing Police and Crime Commissioners in the provinces. The Met is now governed by the Mayor of London's Office for Policing and Crime. The Mayor of London is thus the metropolitan equivalent of a provincial Police and Crime Commissioner. So the commissioner of the Met now has effectively two overseers, the mayor and the Home Secretary, although the latter is no longer directly involved in the governance of the force beyond appointing the commissioner.

The governance arrangements for the City of London Police are similarly unique. The police service is governed by and accountable to the city's Court of Common Council, consisting of elected aldermen and "Common Councillors," via its Police Committee. The legislation introducing Police and Crime Commissioners did not change this.

Beginning in the 1990s some jurisdictions in Canada and some in Australia began to rewrite their Police legislation, introducing new institutions and consequent distributions of authority over the Police. Canada has protected the operational independence of its Police through a system of appointed Police Services Boards[3] in every province except Quebec. The Boards are composed of elected politicians and appointed independent members. They exist at provincial, regional, and municipal levels. Their powers are limited to approving Police budgets and setting priorities for public safety. They are explicitly excluded from directing Police chiefs "with respect to specific operational decisions or with respect to the day-to-day operations of the force" (Ontario Police Services Act 1990, s. 31(4)). The Ontario Act further prohibits Board members from issuing directions to any police personnel except chiefs. Since savvy chief officers often encourage board members to visit police facilities and "ride along" on police operations, it is hard to see how this prohibition can be strictly observed.

The Australian state of New South Wales introduced a Police Board to govern the state police service, and as a buffer between the service and the police minister, in 1983, but it was abolished thirteen years later. A similar board was established in the Australian state of Victoria in 1992, but it too was abolished seven years later.

New Zealand established a State Services Commission (SSC) to replace its former Public Service Commission in 1962. The New Zealand Police, however, was outside the remit of the SSC, as this was considered necessary to preserve the independence of the police. In 1988, the *State Sector Act* gave the SCC responsibility for reviewing the performance of all departmental heads in the public service, including the commissioner of police. In 2008 s. 14 of the new *Policing Act* specifically made the State Services Commissioner responsible for managing the process of the appointment of the commissioner and any deputy commissioner, and required him or her to "provide advice on nominations for Commissioner and any Deputy Commissioners to the Prime Minister and the Minister" of Police. The SCC and its commissioner have thus assumed a significant role in the governance of the police in New Zealand (Stenning 2007, 230-3, 237; Yska 2013, chapter 8).

4. Court decisions

In Britain the delineation of the principles that define the police-government relationship has occurred more often through the decisions of higher courts than through legislative enactment. The most influential was the decision of Lord Denning delivered in *R. v. Commissioner of Police*, ex parte Blackburn in 1968, as described in the preceding chapter. This decision has been cited with approval in later English decisions as well as by higher courts in other Commonwealth jurisdictions, including the Canadian Supreme Court and superior courts in Australia and New Zealand.

In the United States and India, courts have historically played minimal roles in delineating principles governing the police-government relationship, although a significant exception occurred in India. In 2006 the Supreme Court ruled on a petition by a retired police officer asking it to direct the central and state governments to "frame a new Police Act on the lines of the model Act drafted by the National Police Commission [1977-81] in order to ensure that the police is made accountable essentially and primarily to the law of the land and the people." In its decision the Supreme Court set out seven directives, the first of which stated unequivocally that the police were to be independent of political pressure (Prakash Singh v. Union of India, 2006-07)[4]:

(1) The State Governments are directed to constitute a State Security Commission in every State to ensure that the State Government does not exercise unwarranted

influence or pressure on the State police and for laying down the broad policy guidelines so that the State police always acts according to the laws of the land and the Constitution of the country.

The second directive required governments to establish independent, merit-based appointment processes for senior police executives and guarantee them minimum two-year tenure.

Indian state governments have been slow and in some cases obstructive in implementing these directives. A dozen years after the original decision was handed down, most state governments have still not implemented most of the Court's directives:

> The cumulative picture that emerges is one of a political executive that does not wish to let go of its firm grip on policing and perhaps also does not have the capacity to exercise a more guiding role. Rather than ensuring legitimate monitoring and guidance by the executive, the present SSC's [State Security Commissions] perpetuate the executive's control over the police. Unless this changes, the police will be held back from becoming a people-oriented police service for the twenty-first century.(Nagar 2014)

In the United States, two initiatives have been developed that supplement political oversight. One is the use of "consent decrees" initiated by the US Department of Justice to address "patterns and practice" that systematically violate civil or constitutional rights. These decrees, supervised by federal judges, require stipulated changes in the operations of designated police forces. By December 2014 nineteen police forces had been cited in this way. A second initiative has been the creation of civilian review boards in over one hundred cities that receive, sometimes investigate, and more rarely adjudicate complaints from the public about the behavior of officers. Although their numbers have grown steadily since the early 1990s, they remain very unpopular with police, especially the unions. The public, too, has misgivings about their competence and their representativeness. Unlike Canada, the United States has created only a handful of independent boards to protect the police from political interference or to monitor organizational performance with respect to public safety.

5. Terms of appointment

Historically, police chiefs in all six countries were appointed for indefinite terms but held office "at pleasure," thus being vulnerable to arbitrary dismissal. This ensured political control over them. In the twentieth-century tenure "at pleasure" came to be recognized in several jurisdictions as undesirable and requiring reform. Some jurisdictions introduced legislation requiring that police chiefs be given some security of tenure, at least until a stipulated retirement age, and that they could only be dismissed "for cause" established under procedurally acceptable processes.

By the 1980s, however, when "New Public Management" concepts were gaining acceptance, this too came to be regarded as unacceptable (Walsh and Kieron 1995). Led by New Zealand, the practice grew of making fixed-term rather than "permanent" appointments of senior public servants, who were required to sign performance agreements and were required to submit to regular performance reviews. Furthermore, heads of government departments and agencies in Australia, Britain, and New Zealand came to be treated as service providers and were required to sign on to periodic "Purchase Agreements" under which their "deliverables" were specified. Police chiefs in these countries are now appointed for fixed terms, typically of three or five years. This has been less true in Canada, even rarer in the United States where the majority of chiefs have no contract at all (PERF, Private communication 2014), and nonexistent in India.

The introduction of these reforms to the terms and conditions of police chief appointments, beginning in the late 1980s and early 1990s, has had dramatic implications for more recently appointed police chiefs' perceptions of their political "independence."

Conclusion

The countries on which our research is based have important similarities in context as well as notable differences. They are all robust democracies with respect for the rule of law and institutions of representative government. Four of the six (Australia, Canada, India, and the United States) have foundational written constitutions, and all have laws and judicial precedents that defend human rights and liberties. They are diverse ethnically but respect differences and work hard to accommodate them. They have independent media and energetic civil societies. All except India belong to the "developed" world.

In terms of differences, three countries are among the geographically largest in the world (Australia, Canada, and the United States), one is medium (India), and two are small (New Zealand and the Britain). Densities of population range from very low in four (Australia, Canada, New Zealand, and the United States), one is medium (Britain), and one is among the highest in the world (India). Australia, Canada, and India are federations, which has the effect of concentrating authority over policing at the level of their constituent states/ provinces/territories. The United States too is a federation but, like Canada, it has distributed policing authority to the lowest level of government—counties/regions and munici-palities. This distribution of police jurisdictions across our sample means that the scale of governmental supervision also varies enormously. Finally, four of the countries (Australia, Britain, Canada, New Zealand) have in recent times created institutions to mediate the relations between government and police. They have varied, however, in coverage, form, and authority. The United States has a few; India has none at all.

The differences in governance both institutionally and contextually are so great that it raises the question of whether experience in police governance can be validly compared among these countries. What works well in one place may not work well in another. The success of a particular set of governance institutions in one country may depend on context rather than a transferable governance logic. Comparing governance experience across so diverse and small a set of countries may violate a fundamental principle of social science analysis, namely, "other things must be equal." We will explore this issue in chapter 8 in which we examine the factors associated with differences in the experiences of police governance in the six countries.

Notes

1. The data in van Dijk, van Kestren, and Smit (2007), are from the International Crime Victimization Survey, but India is not included. The data in the Indian National Crime Records Bureau report are police-recorded data, so are not comparable, as well as being much more recent. There are no readily available published comparative country-by-country data on different categories of crime (e.g., violent crime or property crime).
2. The province of Newfoundland and Labrador joined the Canadian confederation in 1949.
3. They have different names in different provinces. Boards of police commissioners were first introduced as governing authorities for city police forces in the colony of Upper Canada, now the province of Ontario, in the mid-nineteenth century (Stenning 1981).
4. Accessible online at http://judis.nic.in/supremecourt/imgst. aspx?filename=28072

References

Bowman, A., and R. Kearney. 2011. "Second-Order Devolution: Data and Doubt." Publius 41(4): 563–85.

Burczycka, M. 2013. *Police Resources in Canada 2012.* Catalogue No. 85–225-X. Ottowa: Statistics Canada.

Fearon, James D. 2003. "Ethnic and Cultural Diversity by Country." *Journal of Economic Growth* 8(2): 195–222.

India, National Crime Records Bureau. 2013. *Crime in India 2012: Statistics.* New Delhi: Ministry of Home Affairs.

Nagar, A. 2014. *State Security Commissions: Bringing Little to the Table—A Study of Police Oversight in India.* New Delhi: Commonwealth Human Rights Initiative.

Stenning, P. 1981. *Police Commissions and Boards in Canada.* Toronto, ON: Centre of Criminology, University of Toronto.

Stenning, P. 2007. "The Idea of the Political 'Independence' of the Police: International Interpretations and Experiences." In *Police and Government Relations: Who's Calling the Shots?,* edited by Beare, M. and T. Murray, 183-256. Toronto: University of Toronto Press.

Queensland, Commission of Inquiry into Possible Illegal Activities and Associated Police Misconduct (Fitzgerald Inquiry). 1989. *Report.* Brisbane, QLD: Government Printer.

US Advisory Commission on Intergovernmental Relations 1999. *Annual Report.* Washington, DC: U.S. Government Printing Office.

Van Dijk, J., J. van Kestren, and P. Smit. 2007. *Criminal Victimization in International Perspective.* The Hague: WODC.

Walsh, K., and W. Kieron. 1995. *Public Services and Market Mechanisms: Competition, Contracting and the New Public Management.* Basingstoke: Macmillan.

Yska, R. 2013. *100 Years of Public Service: A Centenary Celebration of New Zealand's State Services Commission.* Wellington: N.Z. State Services Commission. Accessed September 29, 2015. http://www.ssc.govt.nz/sites/all/files/centenary.pdf

Part II

The Practice of Police Governance

5

Governing at the Cutting Edge

Disagreements between politicians and police executives come thick and fast in some countries; in others they are rare to almost nonexistent. In this chapter we examine the character of the relationship between politicians and police chiefs as they manage their respective obligations in governance. First, we identify the protagonists–politicians and police. Second, we examine national differences in the salience and content of disagreements about governance. And third, we describe the ways in which politicians and chiefs conduct this uniquely democratic dance, distinguishing processes of disagreement by the way in which they are resolved.

Our descriptions of the conduct and resolution of governance disagreements draw largely, though not exclusively, on the testimony of police chiefs. We could find information from public sources about how often serious disagreements occur and the issues involved. This is very rarely true for information about how disagreements are conducted and resolved because they are often conducted privately. In order to describe the processes, it is necessary to talk to participants. Our account, therefore, is very much the police perspective.

The comparisons among the six countries will be inferential and imprecise because unless an interaction becomes visible publicly or the protagonists report privately, it is difficult for outsiders to determine whether the relationship was contentious or harmonious. Indeed, even visible disagreements can create a distorted impression about the long-term character of the relationship. They may be one-offs or simply allegations exaggerated by the media. On the other hand, the few visible incidents may represent only the tip of an iceberg whose greater bulk lies out of sight. Even the private characterizations of the relationship by involved politicians and chiefs come with bias. One chief noted that requests from politicians were very common but because he felt confident in ignoring or refusing them, "I was never put under pressure to do [them], and if pressure was intended I didn't see it." Another chief said that for the same reason he never worried about whether directions were "inappropriate." He did as he thought right and drew lines where he liked. Both politicians and chiefs are also unlikely to be forthcoming if they have customarily deferred to the other rather than contesting justifiable issues of accountability and interference. Accommodation is sometimes wise, but it may also appear as weakness. No one wants to look as if they "caved."

We focus our analysis on disputes that arise out of the roles each need to play in democratic governance, namely, holding the police to account and enforcing the law without partisanship. Disagreements arise when politicians become too directive and when police resist direction or oversight. Unpacking these categories further, political directiveness becomes particularly troublesome when it introduces partisanship into the following kinds of decisions:

1. Personnel, thus undermining merit
2. Criminal investigations, undermining the rule-of-law
3. Operational strategy and deployment, undermining professional expertise

Resistance to accountability, on the other hand, becomes most troublesome when police do the following:

1. Deny the authority of politicians to hold them to account
2. Fail to inform political supervisors as expected
3. Refuse to explain what they have done, or provide misleading explanations

We will examine the frequency and substance of these six kinds of disputes across our sample. They do not, however, exhaust all the issues over which politicians and police may quarrel.

The Protagonists

Chiefs have to deal with a wide variety of politicians, some directly in the chain of command, others simply resident in their jurisdiction, and still others from higher levels of governmental authority. Who are the politicians to whom the police must be most responsive? There are three kinds: (1) directly elected, (2) appointed from the ranks of the elected, and (3) appointed non-elected. With the third category, the realm of "politician" has expanded, for reasons that will be explained.

The best examples of *directly elected* political supervisors of police are mayors and city councils in the United States, state Chief Ministers and members of state legislatures (MLAs) in India, and Police and Crime Commissioners in New Britain. The elected members of the executive are generally more active in supervision than members of councils and legislatures. India is an exception to this, especially when executive power is challenged by a powerful legislative opposition.

Appointed-elected politicians are those elected to public office who are then chosen by an elected chief executive to supervise police. This occurs in countries that have parliamentary forms of government, which includes all the countries except the United States. In Australia, India, and

New Zealand these supervisors are commonly called police ministers and are members of the cabinet of their respective governments. In Canadian provinces, supervision is formally shared with elected ministers. Their titles vary from province to province–for example, Solicitor-General and minister of police. In Old Britain, the central government's Home Secretary was assigned by law to carry its police portfolio, a recognized part of the tripartite system of local police supervision. In New Britain, the Home Secretary retains a supervisory role, but shares it with the new Police and Crime Commissioners. Supervision of the London Metropolitan Police is the responsibility of the Mayor's Office of Policing and Crime (MOPAC), which is chaired by a deputy to the mayor.

Appointed non-elected supervisors are individuals appointed by elected governments and designated by law specifically to oversee the police. The best examples are members of supervising boards, such as so-called "independent" members of Old Britain's Police Authorities or Canadian Police Services Boards. Some of the members may be elected officials appointed to the post. Others may be non-elected. They are referred to as independent members. In the United States, city managers are non-elected supervisors who are appointed by mayors and councils. Although all of these are non-elected, they are appointed "politically."

All these types of politicians sometimes supervise through members of their staffs. Sometimes, too, staff officers act completely on their own, in effect assuming the authority of their bosses. This is particularly prevalent in India. Some politicians, especially those not in the chain of command, may publicly "demand" something or other be done even though they have no directing authority whatsoever. Regarded by chiefs as "show boating," this practice nonetheless sends messages that chiefs may feel they should not disregard.

Even more subtly, politicians plant stories, allegations really, in the media about police activity, compelling the police to respond with information they might otherwise prefer to withhold. As a former Canadian chief said:

> When you occupy a high-profile public office like that of police chief, some people are bound to take a few shots at you. Unfortunately, what they say can end up in print, on the radio, and TV, even when none of it is true. People are free to file a statement of claim that may contain the most vicious lies. They can accuse you and members of your family of anything they want, and all they have to do is qualify it to say the allegations are not proven. But the damage gets done. (Fantino 2007, 250)

In the memoirs of chief police officers from all six countries, this kind of anonymous influence is mentioned many times (Blair 2009; Dhillon 2013; Harrington 1999; Mark 1978; Nixon 2011; Whitrod 2001). Of all the pressures on police chiefs, it is probably the most detested. In the unforgettable words of Christine Nixon, former chief commissioner of the Victoria Police in Australia: "The modern media is a voracious, unforgiving, unpredictable, and unforgetting beast. One minute vacuous and silly; the next serious probing." (Nixon 2011, 208)

Pinpointing the police players in the accountability drama is much easier than with their political supervisors. They are the chief officers of police agencies. Of particular importance are those with day-to-day responsibility for law enforcement and public safety. By country, they are as follows:

- Australia–State, Commonwealth, and Territory commissioners of police
- Canada–municipal and regional chiefs, and chief constables, and provincial and RCMP commissioners

- India-state directors-general, district superintendents, and station-house commanders
- New Zealand-the national commissioner
- Old and New Britain-chief constables of provincial police services, and commissioners of the Metropolitan Police and the City of London Police
- United States-municipal, county, and State Police commanders

These designations will be familiar to most readers, with the possible exception of India. According to the Indian constitution, authority for police organization, support, and management is delegated to its thirty-four states and territories. Within these commands, authority is devolved to ranges and districts. Each of these is commanded by a member of the Indian Police Service (IPS), which is a nationally selected and trained officer corps. After graduating from the national police academy, IPS officers are assigned to particular states for the rest of their careers, although they may be assigned elsewhere temporarily, including to national agencies.

Directive Interference by Politicians

How prevalent are situations where politicians have intruded in some way that is considered unacceptable by chiefs? What are the issues involved?

We rank the countries from most to least politically intrusive as follows: India, United States, Australia, Canada, New Zealand, and Old Britain. Before 2012 Britain would have ranked with New Zealand but its position is currently unclear due to the dramatic change made in accountability structures. New Zealand, Old Britain, Canada, and Australia are a distinct group with small differences among them compared with the United States, India, and, perhaps New Britain. Although the United States and India are distinct from the first group, there is a large gap between the United States and India, not in India's favor. What is the state of play in each country that justifies our ranking?

It is more informative to begin by describing the country with the most egregious interference by politicians than the country with the least in order to establish a baseline for the kind of overreaching that other countries have avoided. Trying to describe countries with the least amount of unacceptable political direction is like trying to describe a dog that didn't bark.

Referring to our template of inappropriate directions, Indian politicians intrude into all aspects of police management from hiring, promotion, and assignment to criminal investigations and day-to-day operations. In the words of one prominent police officer, "Unfortunately, the police leadership has succumbed to political dictates and has become completely malleable" (Bedi 2009). Or, as another said, "Under the present dispensation, the political executive has a vice-like grip over the police and dictates how the latter will and will not act" (Raghavan 2012). Particularly at senior ranks, tenure in posts is likely to be short. In Madhya Pradesh State, one of India's largest states, the average tenure of the Director General of Police from 1982 to 2012 was one year and one month. Thirteen of the twenty-five DGPs have served less than one year. This is not unusual in India.

Political influence has created what one retired police officer has called a "transfer industry," where personnel decisions are made on the basis of money, partisanship, or personal loyalty. Politicians ask police to file false charges against political opponents, stop investigations against supporters, and suppress reports of crime. R. K. Raghavan, the former Director of India's Central Bureau of Investigation has written, "This is why police investigations in the states are a joke, especially when the ruling party members are suspected of illegal conduct and need to be probed" (Raghavan 2013b). It is not an exaggeration to say that India has two justice systems–the constitutional and the political. Finally, politicians intervene directly in police operations, giving orders wherever advantage can be gained by responding to requests from important constituents. They exert control at all command levels, from state Directors-General of Police to non-commissioned police station commanders.

Of course the independence of the Indian police is not violated every place every day. Many officers tell stories of refusing improper requests and not being punished. Some testify that they gained respect with government and the political establishment for doing so. But officers who do so understand that they are risking their careers and livelihood. The occasional commander may be brave, but fear dominates the executive ranks. Most appear to have given up.

Our characterization of political directiveness in India may seem extreme, harsh indeed. Sadly, our opinion is supported by daily stories in newspapers and magazines and by public opinion polls. Perhaps the best evidence is the decree issued by India's Supreme Court in 2006, requiring state governments, which control the organization and direction of most of India's police, to enact the reforms suggested by the independent National Police Commission twenty-five years before that would limit political direction. We have described this decision in chapter 4. The Supreme Court's intervention, bypassing both legislative and executive authorities, underscores the desperation felt about the need to limit political interference in the administration of Indian law and justice.

If India represents the worst in terms of political interference with police management, what does the best look like? There are two candidates, New Zealand and Old Britain. In both, direct interference is generally not thought to be an issue. Politicians in both countries understand that any hint of interference in personnel decisions, criminal investigations, and daily operations would be regarded by the public as unacceptable. Police chiefs can deflect pressure by appealing to settled understandings. If needed, they can confidently appeal to more senior politicians for relief or even threaten public exposure.

Since the New Zealand police are a single, national organization, political intervention comes only from the national government, specifically through the police minister or the Prime Minister. Police officials are protected by a national law allocating responsibilities between police and politicians and a tradition of deference to professional opinion.

In Old Britain, chief constables were widely recognized as being in the driver's seat because of the judicial ruling by Lord Denning in the 1969 Blackburn case which effectively defined "operational independence" with respect to "law enforcement" as a legal requirement. As one chief constable said, it made chief constables accountable only to the Queen, God, and themselves (St. Johnston 1978, 9).

In the Old British system, local politicians from town and county councils and members both on and off the Police Authorities would be directive, as one chief constable said, in a "British way" by asking questions that contained veiled suggestions. Local politicians accepted the line of demarcation without getting "raw" with the chief constable. They and members of the public also felt free to call attention to problems that they felt needed attention, such as unregulated school-crossings, rowdy bars, and, ubiquitously, "dog fowling" on public paths. In rural areas, chief constables confronted vociferous concern about crime and disorder attributed to "travellers" (Gypsies).

Directiveness appears to have been more intrusive from central government politicians, especially as expressed through the Home Office, one of the legs in the tripartite system. Chief constables cite attempts by the Home Office to enforce the law enforcement priorities of the ruling party, or to soft pedal an investigation damaging to the party, or simply to ask for information that would have been inappropriate to give. Several chief constables had occasion to say, "I'm not having this conversation with you." As police scholar Robert Reiner has argued, operational independence was so well understood that chief constables could simply assert it (Reiner 1991).

In New Britain, however, directiveness seems to be very much in play again. The unwritten understandings of Old Britain have gone, while new ones have not yet solidified through the give-and-take of experience. A political scientist said on the BBC that "Basically, what the Police and Crime Commissioner (PCC) wants, the PCC gets, at least until the next election" (BBC 11 June 13). If the line between policy and operations becomes more blurred, chief constables may not be able to defend their independence by simple assertion as in the past, but will need to marshal public support. They may have to ask, as one chief constable said, "Who are the friends I need?"

Not far removed from New Zealand and Old Britain on our scale are Australia and Canada. In both countries blatant attempts to direct police with respect to personnel decisions, criminal investigations, or active operations are rare. In the words of a recent Canadian report that would apply to Australia as well, "The matter of police independence may be relatively settled . . ." (Expert Panel on the Future of Canadian Policing Models 2014, 60). Australian and Canadian chief officers are protected by provincial and state legislation stipulating that the day-to-day management is a police responsibility. There are occasional attempts to shape personnel appointments, especially to the senior staff.

Similarly, indirect but strongly felt direction may come from governments and supervising boards through their control of budgets. Although legislation in both countries separates the making of policy from the direction of police management, the boundary is sometimes unclear and sharp disagreements may arise. We discuss this in greater detail at the end of the chapter. As in other democracies, chiefs in both Australia and Canada deal with countless requests about homeless persons, drug markets, property damage, prostitution, double parking, and night-time noise. By and large, these requests are accepted as part of democratic policing and chief officers are willing to engage directly with the people who voice them, as long as they are not couched as directions or instructions.

Between New Zealand, Old Britain, Australia, and Canada, on one hand, where directiveness is reasonably limited, although never out of contention, and India, on the other, where politicians shamelessly intrude, lies the United States. The situation in the United States is today very much as it was portrayed in a textbook on police administration twenty years ago:

> In virtually every large US police jurisdiction, as well as many small ones, police have at one time or another been improperly influenced by partisan politics or, simply, by crooks who have used political office as a means for accumulating personal wealth. (Fyfe et al. 1997, 483)

US chiefs everywhere are on alert about politicians intruding "inappropriately." The director of the Police Executive Research Forum says "This worries police chiefs more than anything" (Wexler, pers. comm., 2013). Directions from politicians about personnel and operational matters are common, although there is considerable variation across the country. In some places, intrusions are rare, based on accepted tradition. Mayors or city managers may say, "You run the department, I'll handle the politics." Or even, "I don't want to be involved in your stuff." In others, interference is constant and chiefs must be prepared to resign if lines are crossed. There are jurisdictions where aspiring chiefs know they should not apply for the top job unless they are willing to accept directions routinely from politicians.

Intrusions are most common with regard to decisions about personnel, especially promotions and assignments. Hiring is governed by and large by state civil services rules. Unless safeguarded in law, politicians may want to hand-pick or at least approve senior staff. Favoritism in assigning police officers to different duties or places is very common, and often appears to be negotiable as long as the officer is as qualified as any other or the assignment does not violate rules established by the police union, such as seniority. In effect, the worst abuses of the old political spoils system have been eliminated, but some politicians would like to bring them back.

The brightest line of separation in responsibilities occurs in the conduct of criminal investigations. Chiefs feel relatively safe in saying that these are off-limits–"Don't even ask." Requests for special treatment for particular persons are not uncommon, however, especially with respect to minor offences, such as public drunkenness or traffic offences. Some politicians ask for information about ongoing investigations or advance notice about raids and inspections of licensed premises. These appear to be resistible.

US chiefs need to be vigilant against intrusions into operational decisions, particularly as they affect the organizational structure of the agency and priorities in law enforcement. Politicians may ask for increased deployments in particular neighborhoods, less attention to favored bars and taverns, or more or less motor vehicle parking enforcement at certain locations.

Altogether, political practice in the United States acknowledges that rules separating politics from policing are important. The content of the rules, however, is very much in play from place to place and depends more on the defensive resolution of chiefs than the forbearance of politicians.

Having compared the frequency and substance of political directiveness among our six countries, we offer two general observations about the independence of the police. First, what police do touches many people one way or another, sometimes significantly, sometimes not; sometimes favorably, sometimes not. Because policing is the most visible face of governmental regulation, democratic politics will always involve issues about it. In each of our countries, police executives excuse requests coming from politicians that reflect concerns of constituents rather than the partisan interests of the politician. The rub, of course, is that intervening on behalf of constituents also enhances the political advantage of politicians. Chiefs understand this; they accept it as part of democracy. But it requires them to negotiate with politicians over boundaries that will always be highly judgmental.

Second, some police chiefs resist intervention in any form and on any issue as a violation of their operational independence. They defend the principle of operational independence as if any accommodation would be the beginning of a slippery slope. Although this may simplify management from their point of view, it violates accountability by refusing to accept reasonable discussion.

Resistance to Accountability by Police

How prevalent are situations where the police have refused oversight? What are the issues involved? Following our template, we looked at instances when the police denied political authority, failed to inform, or were unwilling to explain past actions.

Accountability problems become visible most often when police have failed in some obvious way, such a failing to prevent a serious crime or overusing physical force, and the public wants to assign responsibility. This puts politicians in an awkward position. They are comfortable asking for records and accounts about what went wrong. That is accountability after the fact, which is expected. But they do not want to be held accountable before the fact, that is, held responsible for not having prevented what happened.

The difficult question for politicians, therefore, is how much should police be required to tell them as operations unfold? They do not want to be surprised but they do not want to be held responsible either. It is difficult to formulate principles that guarantee timely forewarning without at the same time implicating politicians in what has gone wrong. It is perhaps only a little cynical to observe that politicians often discover the importance of "operational independence" at moments of crisis. One New Zealand police minister, for instance, became well known for invoking "police independence" to avoid being held accountable in the parliament for police activities. As he put it on one occasion:

> I consider it my duty as Minister to be well briefed on current issues in order that I can make informed decisions on matters of policy, resources, and administration. However, in matters concerning investigative practice, law enforcement decisions, or any of the responsibilities, authorities, or powers within the office of constable, I have no direct involvement in operational policing matters. Those are quite rightly the domain of the Commissioner.[1]

A classic explanation of such a refusal to take political responsibility for police law enforcement activities is that of then Canadian Prime Minister Pierre Trudeau in responding to a journalist's question about some apparently illegal activities of the R.C.M.P. The journalist asked him "just how ignorant does a minister have to be before, at the very least, some responsibility is applied to the advisers who seem to have kept him ignorant?" His response was characteristically blunt:

> I have attempted to make it quite clear that the policy of this government and, I believe, the previous governments in this country, has been that they–indeed, the politicians who happen to form the Government–should be kept in ignorance of the day-to-day operations of the police force and even of the security force. I repeat that it is not a view that is held by all democracies, but it is our view, and it is one we stand by. Therefore, in this particular case, it is not a matter of pleading ignorance as an excuse. It is a matter of stating, as a principle, that the particular minister of the day should not have a right to know what the police are constantly doing in their investigative practices, in what they are looking at and what they are looking for, and in the way in which they are doing it
>
> That is our position. It is not one of pleading ignorance to defend the Government. It is one of keeping the Government's nose out of the operations of the police force, at whatever level of government.
>
> On the criminal law side, the protections we have against abuse are not with the Government, they are with the courts.

Trudeau was strongly criticized for this view in the report of a Commission of Inquiry which was set up to investigate this police illegality (Canada, Commission of Inquiry. . . . 1981: Vol. II, chapter 10). We note, however, how closely Trudeau's statement reflects Lord Denning's opinion in the English *Blackburn* case.

The upshot is that issues of accountability are less likely to become visible because politicians complain than because an attentive public does. The custodians of police independence are the police themselves; the custodians of police accountability are the public and the media.

In India and the United States, accountability is a matter of substantial public concern, but the solutions suggested differ. The Indian police are thought to be accountable only to politicians whose oversight is unpredictable and motivated by bribery and electoral self-interest. Pressure for reform comes from people outside the political establishment, such as NGOs, the media, and retired police officers. Indian political parties have shown no interest whatsoever in increasing accountability over the police except to themselves. In the absence of either effective judicial or political oversight, the Indian Supreme Court alone among government agencies has addressed the accountability issue. In its 2006 judgment, it required the states of India to implement the reforms suggested by the National Police Commission in 1981.

In the United States, concern about accountability arises periodically in many places. Concern has focused mainly on the misdeeds of individual officers, such as the use of force, racial profiling, and corruption, and not on the general performance of the police in controlling crime. Americans are unsure about how to increase accountability. Although they may be disappointed in the failure of existing institutions to prevent misbehavior, they have not given up on political oversight. The automobile bumper-sticker "Support Your Local Police" is more than a plea for local control; it demonstrates continued faith in the politics of small scale.

In sum, Indians and Americans are very concerned about holding the police to account either for organizational performance or individual behavior. The Indians have formulated but not implemented a set of solutions similar to Canada's. Americans question the adequacy of political oversight but have not yet given up on elective politics. They are experimenting with the various forms of oversight (political, judicial, executive, independent), their location (national, state, local), and the scope of their charge (organizational, individual). As usual in the United States' complex federal system with over seventeen thousand police forces authorized by fifty state laws and countless local governments, nothing is straightforward and reform is piecemeal.

Accountability, and the processes through which it is achieved, has been transformed in New Zealand and Australia, and to a lesser extent in Britain and Canada, as a result of the adoption of "new public management" styles of governance, with their stipulations about purchase agreements, performance contracts, citizen's charters, etc. which we discuss further in chapter 8. Our interviewees in these countries have been virtually unanimous in asserting that expectations and demands for accountability have significantly increased since these governmental reforms were introduced in the late 1980s and 1990s. Modern job advertisements for chiefs, with their stipulations about managerial expertise, performance indicators and implementation of government policies and priorities, clearly reflect these developments.

For all these reasons, ranking our countries with respect to accountability is difficult. The issue seems to have been settled and relatively uncontroversial in Old Britain. Concern about whether the institutional arrangements for ensuring accountability were adequate–the tripartite system–was minimal. With the introduction of elected PCCs, police accountability has again become a matter of high politics. Very unlike Old Britain, police accountability has been hugely controversial in India and the United States, although not to the same degree. In the middle of the continuum are Australia, Canada, and New Zealand, where the issue has transformed but only occasionally becomes controversial.

The Processes of Disagreement

The process of disagreeing is the same in all six countries, although the manner in which political requests are communicated varies considerably–direct orders, strong advice, suggestions, opinions, pointed questions, and hints. Generally, when a political player suggests an unacceptable course of action, the police chief asks for a reconciliation of views. If the politician agrees, discussions then ensue, usually in private. Discussions may become public, and hence visible, when private discussion fails. In countries where the public has been sensitized to the issue of political influence, the threat by chiefs to go public is a powerful inducement to compromise. When this happens, the dispute remains invisible, which is another reason why the extent of disagreement about governance between countries is difficult to estimate reliably.

We explore the processes of disagreement by their manner of resolution. There are four: (1) irreconcilable differences, producing a complete rupture of the relationship; (2) political deference to the police perspective; (3) police deference to the political perspective; and (4) negotiated compromise. There are other ways of categorizing processes of disagreement. One already discussed is whether breakdowns occur privately or publicly. Another is the speed with which disagreements arise, such as flashing unexpectedly into prominence or burning slowly over time. The "Bright" (1971) and "Mitchell" (1978) reports in South Australia (South Australia, Commission of Inquiry 1971; South Australia Commission of Inquiry 1978) and the "Arar Commission" report in Canada (Canada, Commission of Inquiry 2006) are examples of "flashpoint" breakdowns. The "Fitzgerald Report" (Queensland, Commission of Inquiry 1989), the Queensland Criminal Justice Commission report (1992), and the New South Wales Parliament Joint Select Committee report (Duncan 1993a, 1993b) are examples of "slow burns."

Slow burns provide more opportunity to take remedial action, provided, of course, that police chiefs and politicians are able to recognize the trajectory.

Examples of the four types of processes based on the manner of resolution can be found in each country of our sample. There are, however, important differences among them. Accordingly, we have selected examples from the countries where they are most common. For irreconcilable differences, the United States, India, and Australia; for political deference, Old Britain and Canada; for police deference, New Zealand and Australia; and for negotiated compromise, all six.

Irreconcilable Differences

In the United States, firings and resignations are not rare. An Internet search shows many. Police chiefs say they must be constantly on the alert against encroachments and must be willing to draw lines, even at the risk of being fired. In a survey of forty-two US chiefs, 80 percent said they had significant conflict, some with threats of being fired (Johnson 2012). The US chiefs we interviewed mentioned the following requests that they rejected:

- Crime policies promised during election campaigns
- Strength of deployments in particular neighborhoods
- Making or not making arrests during public protests
- Appointments to senior posts
- Assignment of officers to particular duties or shifts
- Prosecuting a city manager or county executive
- Cutting money for a crime prevention program
- Disciplining or not disciplining an officer
- Closing a police station
- Closing a road
- Accompanying funeral processions
- Campaigning for the mayor
- Centralizing all media communication by the police through the mayor's office

In one city an elected member of the County Board accused the chief of "overreacting" when he allowed the police helicopter to shine its spotlight into a middle-class neighborhood while chasing a fleeing suspect. The chief said, "I declined to either accept the premise of his demand nor accede to it. The conversation degenerated from there."

While many directives involve relatively small matters, some can be hugely sensitive. In Miami, Florida, federal agents raided a house in order to seize a young Cuban boy (Alian Gonzalez) and deport him to members of his family living in Cuba. The case was closely followed by media nationwide. After the raid the mayor demanded that the city manager fire the police chief for failing to inform him about the impending raid. When the city manager refused to do so, the mayor did. The chief then resigned arguing that he did not deserve to be fired because law enforcement was an operational matter and the federal agents had in any case only notified him one hour before the raid (*Washington Post* 2000). In another case, an African-American mayor requested that a black officer be promoted to deputy chief. The chief, who was white, refused and prevailed when he threatened to resign and reveal the race-based favoritism.

Chiefs are occasionally fired outright for enforcing the law against the wishes of politicians. This happened to a chief in a small town on the east coast of the United States when he insisted against the wishes of the town council on following his stated policy of never "fixing" (excusing) citations for traffic infractions. Another was fired for refusing the mayor's request not to enforce a town ordinance requiring the police to tow and impound vehicles of people arrested for possession of drugs found in a vehicle (McDevitt and Field 2010).

Australia too has had lots of contentious drama across its six State Police services. Perhaps the most celebrated was the resignation of Commissioner Ray Whitrod in Queensland in 1976 after repeated attempts by the state's Premier to sup-press investigations and, the last straw, to appoint an assistant commissioner over Whitrod's objection. The irony is that the assistant commissioner (Terry Lewis) who was later promoted to commissioner was arrested and sent to prison for corrup-tion and mismanagement (Fitzgerald Commission 1989; Stenning 2007, 215–7). Commissioner Salisbury in South Australia was also dismissed in the late 1970s for misleading the Chief Secretary in response to a request for information. In a very recent example, Victorian Chief Commissioner Overland resigned in 2011 when the Ombudsman found he had released misleading crime statistics favorable to govern-ment immediately before an election.

In New South Wales the shoe was on the other foot. The police minister was forced to resign in 1992 because he had misled the Parliament about the police's accountability. The minister had claimed, incorrectly, that the commissioner had not kept him informed about the attempted suicide of a young man in a police cell that had resulted in brain damage (New South Wales Parliament, Joint Select Committee, 1993).[2]

In India, firings and resignations are rare but the replace-ment and re-assignment of senior commanders are very common. The average tenure in office for a state Director General of Police is rarely over two years and in some states has been as short as six months. Referring to the 2006 injunction by the Supreme Court that state governments implement corrective reforms, the retired director of India's Central Bureau of Investigation wrote recently, "Security of tenure for police officers in key posts was the bedrock on which that order rested, and this is precisely what has been violated uninhibitedly by a majority of states" (Raghavan 2013a). Commanders of police stations, the lowest level of command, are particularly vulnerable to transfer when local politicians search for officers who are willing to use their powers of arrest, bail, and investigation against political adversaries.

Political Deference

In Old Britain, inappropriate requests for police action of some sort were very common but chief constables felt confident about accepting or rejecting them as they chose. Politicians and the public alike accepted the need for operational independence as articulated by the chief constables. Politicians knew that if chief constables ran up the "bloody flag" of operational independence, they would lose in the court of public opinion. The political culture of police governance was so well set that chief constables could warn off would-be political intruders with the threat of exposure.

Political deference seems to have occurred more readily at local levels in Old Britain with Police Authorities and local council members than at the national level, in particular with the Home Office. Many chief constables recount instances when the Home Secretary and even the Prime Minister asked for information about criminal investigations, wanted investigations stopped, or directed actions be taken in ways the chief constable thought unacceptable. Defiance by chief constables of national politicians seems to have required a higher degree of confrontation than with local ones, along the lines of "I'm not having this conversation with you" or simply going ahead for reasons the chief constable indicated he or she was willing to defend publicly. Chief constables report that they solicited the support of their local Police Authorities against directives from the Home Office. In sum, Lord Denning's 1968 strictures about the total operational independence of Chief constables with respect to "law enforcement" became a bulwark unassailable by politicians.

Early this century noticeable cracks in the separation began to emerge, especially concerning the London Metropolitan Police. Ian Blair, commissioner from 2005 to 2008, was the first commissioner to resign in over one hundred years. He did so after the mayor said publicly that he had "lost confidence" in his leadership. Two years later Commissioner Stephenson also resigned when the Home Secretary criticized him for failing to inform him that the Met had hired a former member of the staff of the News International as media advisor while the Met was investigating the newspaper for illegal phone tapping (Stenning 2011). Obviously, old expectations about the way criticism of the commissioner of the Met were to be expressed have been upset.

In Canada, requests from politicians are for the most part handled privately, with chiefs reporting that they have no problem rejecting them and having their explanations accepted. Requests come by and large from members of Police Service Boards. Firings and resignations are very rare. One big city chief said that his board never insisted on anything over his professional advice. "Unless I'm looney, I'm OK." Another said that threatening to "out" an inappropriate request to the media was like giving the politician "both barrels to the chest." There was one highly publicized exception– the unprecedented resignation in 2006 of the commissioner of the RCMP for giving misleading and contradictory testimony to parliament in the Arar Affair (Stenning 2011, and recounted in chapter 2).

The peaceable façade in Old Britain and Canada does not mean that political deference is easily earned. When a British chief constable was directed by the Home Secretary to "step up the action against picketing" in a local industrial dispute, he asked for the order in writing and never heard from the Home Office again. From time to time, Canadian chiefs too have had to play "hard-ball." Some chiefs state their ground rules during the hiring process. Others recount blunt conversations along the lines of "Never try to influence me again on an issue like this or I'll take it to the press." Others say they have to remind members of their Police Service Boards about the rules laid down in provincial Police Acts. This is not because boards are being willful but more often because some of their members are new to their role. Sometimes relations can become personal and bitter. As one chief said, depending on personal dynamics they can move from deference to "Armageddon" in a heartbeat.

Political deference also occurs in the United States, although very unevenly from place to place. The mayor of one fortunate chief said, "I don't want to be involved in your stuff. If problems arise, fix them. I'll hold you to account for how you do it." Many politicians say this initially, but forget when political interests become involved.

Police Deference

All chiefs can recount episodes where they deferred to political directives because it kept politicians happy while not compromising their own integrity. Choosing one's fights is part of the job of a chief police officer. For example, chiefs may prioritize particular concerns about safety, such as drunken driving, because that mission is as justifiable as the alternatives. Indian officers, for example, report acceding to "political" hires as long as the candidates are already on the list of qualified applicants.

The commissioner of the Australian Federal Police was criticized by the Prime Minister's office for saying on TV that the Madrid bombing in March, 2004, was linked to Spain's military involvement in Iraq (Fleming 2004). The government's position was that Australia's participation in Iraq had not increased the risk from terrorism. After a private conversation between the commissioner and Prime Minister, the commissioner retracted his statement, saying his remarks were taken out of context. The media had a field day, alleging undue political influence.

As we noted earlier, the shift toward "new public management" styles of governance in Australia, Canada, New Zealand, and Britain during the late 1980s and 1990s significantly increased both the permissible scope of political influence over public service operations and expectations about accountability. The police were not exempt from this. At the same time, appointments of police commissioners and chiefs began to be fixed-term rather than "permanent" appointments, based in many cases on specific contracts or performance agreements. Our interviewees, especially in Australia and New Zealand, frequently emphasized that the combination of these two reforms has put commissioners in a position in which resisting government demands was much more risky, since doing so would likely result in their contract not being renewed. The balance of power between ministers and commissioners had thus shifted in favor of the politicians.

Despite assurances from the government to the contrary, a greater degree of police deference is precisely what many police officers and observers fear will be required from New Britain's elected PCCs. Indeed, official guidance about the implementation of the authorizing legislation (Police Reform and Social Responsibility Act 2011) is not reassuring. The following language appears in the Policing Protocol Order, 2011,[3] issued by the Home Office and having the force of law. At several places, it states that chief constables shall remain "operationally independent":

The 2011 Act does not impinge on the common law legal authority of the office of constable, or the duty of constables to maintain the Queen's Peace without fear or favor. It is the will of Parliament and Government that the constable shall not be open to improper political interference. (Paragraph 12)

Chief Constables are charged with the impartial direction and control of all constables and staff within the police force that they lead. (Paragraph 13)

In addition, the PCC must not fetter the operational independence of the police force and the Chief Constable who leads it. (Paragraph 18)

However, the protocol (Paragraph 35) admits that "The concept of operational independence is not defined by statutes, and as HMIC [Her Majesty's Inspectorate of Constabulary] has stated, by its nature, is fluid and context-driven" (Her Majesty's Inspectorate of Constabulary 2010, 17). And

The public accountability for the delivery and performance of the police service is placed into the hands of the PCC on behalf of their electorate. The PCC draws on their mandate to set and shape the strategic objectives of their force area in consultation with the Chief Constables. They are accountable to the electorate; the Chief Constable is accountable to the PCC. (Paragraph 14)

The PCC is specifically empowered to set strategic direction, oversee performance, hold the chief constable to account, decide budget allocations, appoint and fire the chief constable subject to regulations in the Police Act of 1996, maintain an efficient and effective force, and publish information it considers necessary (Paragraph 17). Finally,

In order to respond to the strategic objectives set by the PCC and the wide variety of challenges faced by the police every day, the Chief Constable is charged with the direction and control of the Force and day-to-day management of such force assets *as agreed by the PCC*. (Paragraph 37, emphasis added)

It would be fair to say that with respect to operational independence, current law in New Britain both giveth and taketh away. Nevertheless, the legislation provides a good example of how a legal requirement for a chief and his or her political supervisor to co-operate with each other in developing policy may be specified in legislation. The PCCs are given the ultimate authority to promulgate "police and crime plans" within a year of their appointment, and to vary the content of such plans during their tenure as circumstances are perceived to require. They are authorized to hold chief constables accountable for the effective implementation of these plans, and chief constables in their turn are required to exercise their powers of direction and control over the police service "in such a way as is reasonable to assist the relevant police and crimes commissioner to exercise the commissioner's functions." But the legislation requires that before PCCs finalize their plans, or make any significant variation to them, they must consult with chief constables and their advisory Police and Crime Panels. They must also "have regard to" the national strategic policing requirement that the Home Secretary is authorized to promulgate. If the local Police and Crime Panel submits a report or recommendations in response to a draft plan or proposed variation to it, PCCs must give the panel a response to such report or recommendations, and publish this response. The eventual plan or any variation of it must be published. These provisions reflect a firm commitment to co-operative, consultative, and democratic police governance, which allows maximum opportunity for both police and public discussion of, and input into, policy making, and professional police expertise to be taken into account.

Negotiated Compromise

With the exception of India, negotiated compromise is the most common process for settling disputes among our countries. For example, a member of a Police Board in Canada wanted to apply principles of restorative justice to people arrested in a riot rather than having them prosecuted. After a full board discussion, the chief's law enforcement approach prevailed. In Old Britain a Police Authority acceded to the request of the chief constable for additional money to pursue a criminal investigation. They treated it as an operational matter despite the fact that they controlled the budget.

At local levels in Old Britain, differences were worked out by compromises based on political and operational conditions. The same is true in Australia and New Zealand. One former Australian commissioner described his approach to dealing with unwelcome demands in the following way:

> You need to be apolitical but you need to have enough knowledge about politics to know where not to be, if you know what I mean, in all of that. . . . Find solutions. If they've got a problem find a solution for it. Don't just say no, time and time again. With budgets when money is tight they say "well we've got to try and achieve this," and you could just as easily say "well no we haven't got the money to do it." But you're better off saying "well, if we do this and that and shift this and do that we might be able to actually do that." And then take into account their policies, use a bit of common sense around all of this. Just because they can't give you a direction on something

doesn't mean you ignore it. I think you're a mug if you don't really take into account and consider the realities. Don't go to war with them.

There is an important qualification in believing that disagreements that are reported as negotiated really were. Some terminations and non-renewal of contracts may in fact be dismissals. To save face, chiefs are allowed to resign, often under the excuse that they want "to spend more time with my family."

Conclusion

We have compared six English-speaking democracies with respect to the frequency and content of serious disagreements between politicians and police about management and accountability. Table 5.1 shows both rankings.

Table 5.1

DIRECTIVENESS		ACCOUNTABILITY	
Least	Old Britain	Settled	Old Britain
Intermediate	Australia	Reasonably	Australia
	Canada	settled	Canada
	New Zealand		New Zealand
Most	United States	Unsettled	India,
	India		United States

The obvious conclusion is that the twin goals of nonpartisan supervision and meaningful accountability seem to be linked, as reported by police chiefs. Greater political directiveness is associated with less acceptable accountability. Conversely, the greater the degree operational independence on the part of the police, the more satisfactory accountability seems to be. In our sample, political direction of the police is not considered a preferred way to achieve accountability. The lesson seems to be that people in democracies are dubious about too close an association between politicians and the police even in the interest of accountability. The preferred mechanism at the moment for combining accountability with professionalism is through the creation of a set of institutions that reduce direct contact between politicians and police but at the same time have broad mandates to monitor and set general policies.

Notes

1.   596 New Zealand Parliamentary Debates: 13080–81 (14th November 2001).
2.   For details, see chapter 2.
3.   The Protocol can be accessed online at https://www.gov.uk/ government/uploads/system/uploads/attachment_data/ file/117474/policing-protocol-order.pdf.

References

Bedi, K. 2009. Quoted in Dilip K. Das and Otwin Marenin. *Trends in Policing: Interviews with Police Leaders across the Globe*. Boca Raton, FL: CRC Press.

Blair, I. 2009. *Policing Controversy*. London: Profile Books Ltd.

British Broadcasting Company, June 11, 2013.

Caless, B. 2011. *Policing at the Top: The Roles, Values and Attitudes of Chief Police Officers*. Bristol: The Policy Press.

Canada, Commission of Inquiry into the Actions of Certain Canadian Officials in Relation to Maher Arar. 2006. *Report* (Mr. Justice Dennis, O'Connor, Commissioner). Ottawa, ON: Minister of Public Works & Government Services.

Canada. Commission of Inquiry into Certain Activities of the Royal Canadian Mounted Police (McDonald Inquiry). 1981. Second Report. *Freedom and Security under the Law*. Ottawa: Minister of Supply & Services Canada.

Conway, V. 2010. *The Blue Wall of Silence: The Morris Tribunal and Police Accountability in Ireland*. Dublin, Ireland: Irish Academic Press.

Dhillon, Kirpal. 2013. *Time Present and Time Past: Memoirs of a Top Cop*. New Delhi: Penguin Books.

Duncan, G., NSW Parliament Joint Select Committee upon Police Administration. 1993a. *The Circumstances which Resulted in the*

Resignation of the Honourable E.P. Pickering, MLC, as Minister for Police and Emergency Services: First Report. Sydney: NSW Parliament.

——. 1993b. *Remaining Issues: Final Report.* Sydney: NSW Parliament.

Einstein, S., and M. Amir, eds. 2001. *Policing, Security and Democracy: Special Aspects of Democratic Policing.* The Uncertainty Series. Huntsville, TX: Office of International Criminal Justice.

Expert Panel on the Future of Canadian Policing Models. 2014. *Policing Canada in the 21stcentury – New Policing for New Challenges.* Ottawa: Council of Canadian Academies.

Fantino, Julian, with Jerry Emernic. 2007. *Duty: The Life of a Cop.* Toronto: Key Porter Books Ltd.

Fitzgerald Commission. 1989. *Report of a Commission of Inquiry Pursuant to Orders in Council.* Brisbane, Australia: Government of Queensland.

Fleming, J. 2004. "Les liaisons Dangereuses: Relations between Police Commissioners and their Political Masters." *Australian Journal of Public Administration* 63(3): 60–74.

Fyfe, J. J., J. R. Greene, W. F. Walsh, O.W. Wilson, and R. C. McLaren. 1997. *Police Administration.* New York: McGraw-Hill Companies, Inc.

Goldsmith, A. 2005. "Police Reform and the Problem of Trust." *Theoretical Criminology* 9(4): 443–70.

Hann, R. G., J. H. McGinnis, P. C. Stenning, and A. S. Farson. 1985. "Municipal Police Governance and Accountability in Canada: An Empirical Study." *Canadian Police College Journal* 9(1): 1–85.

Harrington, Penny. 1999. *Triumph of Spirit: An Autobiography by Chief Penny Harrington.* Chicago, IL: Brittany Publications Ltd.

Her Majesty's Inspectorate of Constabulary (HMIC). 2010. *Police Governance in Austerity: HMIC Thematic Report into the Effectiveness of Police Governance.* London: HMIC.

Hills, A. 2006. *Police Commissioners, Presidents, and Accountability in Africa's Security Governance. Paper for Governing Police in Developing Countries.* Los Angeles, CA.

Johnson, J. 2012. "Conflict with Commissioners?" *Police Professional,* August 16, 20–22.

Mark, Sir Robert. 1978. *In the Office of Constable: An Autobiography.* London: William Coillins Sons & Co. Ltd.

McDevitt, Daniel S., and Mark W. Field. 2010. *Police Chief: How to Attain and Succeed in this Critical Position.* Springfield, IL: Charles C. Thomas Publisher.

National Police Commission, India. 1981. *Reports*. New Delhi, India: Government of India.

Nixon, C., and J. Chandler. 2011. *Fair Cop*. Mebourne, Australia: Victory Books.

Queensland, Commission of Inquiry into Possible Illegal Activities and Associated Police Misconduct (Fitzgerald Inquiry). 1989. *Report*. Brisbane: Government Printer.

Queensland, Criminal Justice Commission. 1992. *Report on an Inquiry into Allegations Made by Terence Michael Mackenroth MLA, the Former Minister for Police and Emergency Services, and Associated Matters*. Brisbane: Criminal Justice Commission.

Raghavan, R. K. 2012, October 23. *Delhi Magazine*.

——. 2013a. "Story of a Caged Parrot, Part 2." *Indian Express*, August 17, 2013.

——. 2013b. "Give the Caged Parrot Wings." *Tribune Newspaper*, May 12, 2013.

Reiner, R. 1991. *Chief Constables: Bobbies, Bosses or Bureaucrats?* Oxford: Oxford University Press.

South Australia, Royal Commission [Commissioner: Madam Justice R. Mitchell]. 1978. *Report on the Dismissal of Harold Hubert Salisbury*. Adelaide: Government Printer.

South Australia, Royal Commission on the September Moratorium Demonstration [Commissioner: Mr. Justice Bright]. 1971. *Report*. Adelaide: Government Printer.

Stenning, P. 2007. "The Idea of the Political 'Independence' of the Police: International Interpretations and Experiences." In *Police and Government Relations: Who's Calling the Shots?*, edited by M. Beare and T. Murray, 183–256. Toronto: University of Toronto Press.

——. 2011. "Governance of the Police: Independence, Accountability and Interference." *Flinders Law Journal* 13 (2): 241–67.

St. Johnston, E. 1978. *One Policeman's Story*. Chichester: Barry Rose.

Washington Post, 2000. "A Crisis Unresolved." August 17, 2000.

Whitrod, R. 2001. *Before I Sleep: Memoirs of a Modern Police Commissioner*. St. Lucia, Queensland: Queensland University Press.

6

Advice about Managing

Achieving appropriate accountability over the police in democratic countries depends to some extent on formal regulatory structures. Moreover, no set of structures can guarantee an appropriate balance between accountability and nonpartisan direction in practice. The uncertainties of human interaction, in particular the character and behavior of the people involved, can throw the balance out of kilter. In our interviews with police chiefs we asked what advice they had about making the relationship with supervising politicians work harmoniously in the public interest. Since interaction with politicians begins with the hiring process and extends through their daily interactions on the job, we asked for advice about both phases.

The views of chiefs are, of course, only one side of the story. Politicians undoubtedly have advice as well. For reasons discussed in the introduction, we did not interview politicians. We hope very much that others will. It is possible that the advice from politicians will be less extensive than from chiefs because managing the police is not as central to their responsibilities as managing politicians is to chiefs. Furthermore, politicians not only have a duty to oversee, they must also legislate, setting the rules that executive and judicial agencies follow. Whether politicians and chiefs differ in their attentiveness to police governance should be treated as a hypothesis, with the hope that someone will test it.

Being Hired

The hiring process is an occasion for negotiation between politicians and candidates about roles and agendas. In Australia, chiefs are appointed by governments on the advice of their police ministers, who in turn receive advice from more or less "independent" panels; in Canada, by members of Police Boards and/or supervising ministers; in New Zealand, by the cabinet on the advice of the police minister and the State Services Commissioner; in Old Britain, by Police Authorities with the approval of the Home Secretary; in New Britain, by Police and Crime Commissioners; and in the United States, by local executive officers, primarily mayors and governors. All the appointing authorities are either elected or, if boards, have some elected members. In India, politicians rarely interview candidates, even for top positions in the states or central government police agencies. Selection is made by politicians from a list of officers deemed eligible by seniority and service record prepared by committees consisting of police and civil servants. It is widely accepted that the candidates preferred by appointing politicians are well known to these committees.

In Australia, New Zealand, and New Britain, any negotiation over terms and conditions of appointment is undertaken within the context of approved templates, job descriptions, and performance agreements. Interviewees in Australia indicated that opportunities for negotiation within these parameters are quite limited, but that commissioners who are recruited from abroad, as has happened, may have more room for negotiation. In Canada, practice in this regard varies from province to province. Until recently only the tenure of appointment was negotiated, although problems of shared responsibilities were discussed if there was a local history of conflict. Now initial contracting has become more open ended, with tenure, benefits, and "perks" all on the table. Operational powers are not. The Canadian Association of Police Boards (CAPB) has developed model hiring criteria and procedures.

The most serious at-hiring negotiations take place in the United States. US chiefs believe that great mistakes can be made by the unwary at this stage. Some report having been rejected for appointments for not agreeing to stipulated conditions. Candidates also withdraw applications because of this requirement. In New Britain, negotiations will undoubtedly become more important with the elected Police and Crime Commissioners. Whether they will have the scope of US negotiations is unclear. The Home Secretary will undoubtedly have some influence over both criteria and processes.

In countries where discussions about conditions of service take place, chiefs agree on several points. Candidates should explicitly discuss how appointing politicians see their role. For example, what issues require consultation and, more importantly, approval? Candidates should communicate clearly what they understand the scope of their authority to be and what they would view as unacceptable intrusion. At a minimum, most chiefs agree, candidates should insist on having total responsibility for the selection, promotion, assignment, and discipline of police personnel below the deputy chief level and for direction of operations in the field.

Candidates should discuss the process of interaction with their appointing superior. When does the politician expect to be consulted? How often will meetings take place, and who will prepare the agenda for such meetings? What written communications and briefings are expected? How will differences of opinion be resolved? How comfortable does the politician seem to be at the prospect of forthright disagreement?

Finally, candidates should consider whether they feel comfortable with the crime and law enforcement opinions of the political party in power. They should establish ground rules, if they are not already in place, about when the chief can publicly express views about matters of public safety and law enforcement policy that may not be consistent with government policy. Our interviews suggest that such discussions almost never take place between a prospective commissioner and the police minister in Australia or New Zealand. This is because the ministers are often not directly involved in the selection process but make their hiring recommendations on the basis of recommendations from independent panels. In Britain, any such discussion must take place within limits imposed by the National Policing Plan published by the Home Secretary. The Association of Chief Police Offices (ACPO) has traditionally had some input into these plans. It was recently replaced by a National Police Chiefs' Council.

US chiefs, for whom this topic was especially relevant, suggested a non-confrontational way for having these conversations. Rather than stating bald principles, candidates should ask questions about how decisions are customarily made in the job being offered. In this way they can determine for themselves whether they could function comfortably in the job. Exploration of these issues should not be conducted as hard bargaining, but as open, candid, respectful discussions over a desk or at dinner. Ed Flynn, who has been chief in several US cities, offered a list of questions he asks during interviews (Private communication, 12 March 2013):

(1) To whom do I report? What is the extent of their authority over me and the department?
(2) Who or what boards of commissions also have authority over the agency?
(3) Who is responsible for hiring? What is the hiring process?
(4) Who is responsible for promotion? What is the process?

(5) Who is responsible for discipline? What are the appeal rights of those disciplined?

(6) What is the collective bargaining environment? What are the mandatory subjects in collective bargaining? What are management's rights? Does the chief have input during contract negotiations?

(7) What is my right of assignment? Does the chief control assignment or are they governed by contracts, seniority, or outside agency?

(8) Who controls the budget process? How flexible is the budget process during the course of the fiscal year?

(9) What are the current "hot button" issues and how do the various components of the "authorizing environment" line up on them?

The reference to "contracts" and "collective bargaining" in Flynn's advice reflects the importance of unions in US policing. Limitations on managerial control do not arise only from politicians. In the United States federal system, conditions of employment are regulated under state laws. Savvy candidates need to examine local union and civil service laws to determine how much managerial authority they have.

Managing the Relationship

Turning to advice about managing political relations on the job, chiefs varied across the six countries in their engagement with the topic. US chiefs were very interested in offering advice, clearly regarding the management of politicians as a crucial aspect of their job. They were proud of what they had learned and eager to pass it on. Australian chiefs too were very engaged with the topic, although they were much less worried than Americans about the consequences of disagreement. Canadian chiefs were engaged with the topic, but felt protected more than Australians or Americans by Police Services Boards. Chiefs in Old Britain and New Zealand had the least advice to offer for managing political overseers, apart, of course, from strenuously defending operational independence. New Britain's chiefs are still learning the rules of interaction with the new PCCs.

In New Zealand the practice has developed whereby the police prepare a substantial briefing document for each new incoming police minister. This document typically includes a brief discussion of the accepted respective roles of the minister and commissioner. This is unusual in our sample. One former Australian commissioner told us that a commissioner who gave a minister such unsolicited advice would be considered "a smart-arse."

India, once again, is a special case. Its chief officers offered no advice for their colleagues, other than to be bold and reject over-the-line directions even at the risk of being replaced. Control by politicians seems to be so pervasive and entrenched that advice about managing the relationship is irrelevant.

The advice that chiefs have about tactics for handling politicians is wide ranging, often going in directions we had not anticipated. The main topics were to

- protect your turf,
- anticipate trouble,
- be diplomatic,
- educate staff,
- embrace politics,
- manage appearances,
- take care of yourself.

Protect Your Turf

First and foremost, be clear about your "bottom line." What principles would you not compromise? What would you resign over? Stick to your principles from the beginning. Making even one exception provides a precedent that becomes leverage later on. As one chief said, "do the right things for the right reasons and let the chips fall where they may."

Chiefs should not shy away from discussing issues of respective authority with political supervisors. They should accept responsibility for educating them about the proper scope of oversight. Politicians may overreach as much from ignorance as from a willful assertion of authority. They may be newer at their job of supervision than chiefs are at their job of management. Several Canadian chiefs said that when the composition of their Police Service Board changed, they met privately with new members to discuss critical areas of mutual responsibility, offered tours of facilities and opportunities for observing police work, and discussed how to bring complaints to the chief's attention.

Chiefs need to understand and appreciate what democracy requires of politicians. Politicians are not part of the "evil empire," as one chief said. Chiefs should be respectful to politicians. Politicians work hard; they too have needs. As a British chief said, "grow to know" what concerns different people in the political chain of command. This involves accepting the fact that police chiefs serve under elected governments that have expectations about policy and performance. Politicians make promises about funding, law enforcement priorities, complaint procedures, and transparency. Chiefs must be apolitical in the partisan sense, but they need, as one said, to know "enough about politics to know where not to be."

Anticipate Trouble

Anticipate disagreements and initiate solutions. Rather than waiting for politicians to overreach, chiefs should be alert for the possibility of disagreement and take preventive action. As one US chief said, "If you are not politically savvy, you will soon be a former police chief" (Das and Marenin 2009, p. 16). Furthermore, recognize that politicians react to events, so be alert to situations where a politician will want to appear to be informed and knowledgeable.

Chiefs should not regard negotiating with politicians as taking the first step down a slippery slope of interference.

Inviting discussion is not the same as compromising principle. As one US chief said, "Engage but don't accept direction." Done with mutual respect, discussions are occasions for underlining principles while providing information about how policing works. Chiefs should also insist on regular meetings—"face time"—with their major political supervisor. This requires, as a US chief said, "lots of lunches." In short, relations can be made more comfortable through familiarity.

Never surprise your politician boss. Whether the news is good or bad, make sure the politician knows before anyone else. The corollary is never lie to a supervising politician and never go behind their back. Keep them informed about anything that will likely become public knowledge, such as criticism about police actions, public statements to be made by the chief, sensational crimes, changes in deployment strategies, and meetings with opposition politicians. It is better to overbrief than underbrief about problems. Chiefs must recognize that politicians need to be knowledgeable to do their accountability job intelligently.

Do not "upstage" your supervisor. While chiefs cannot entirely control the attention they get from the media, they can be careful about sharing credit for success. They should avoid appearing to be more important than the politician who has the same, if more general, responsibility. This is not easy because some people are quicker to perceive slights in deference than others. An extreme case was Mayor Rudolph Guiliani's deep resentment of William Bratton's celebrity as police commissioner in New York City in the mid-1990s, particularly after Bratton's picture appeared on the cover of *Time Magazine*. According to Bratton, this prompted Giuliani to obstruct several of his initiatives, leading eventually to Bratton's resignation (Bratton 1998).

Unfair as it may seem, chiefs should share credit but not share blame. They should be prepared to take responsibility for things that go wrong, to "take the hit" for the political administration, remembering, as one chief said, that "our mud splashes on them." A US chief wryly observed that when there was good news to announce, there was a team at the microphone; when there was bad news, he stood alone.

Be Diplomatic

Because you are in an ongoing relationship with your political supervisor, treat him or her with respect. Occasional disagreements are unavoidable, but the relation must endure to manage new challenges. Recognize honest differences, search for compromises, and choose your battles wisely.

Do not be unduly rigid in disagreements. Some issues are worth fighting for, others are not. Chiefs must learn to calculate costs and benefits, when to push back and when to "eat it." Furthermore, an antagonist one day may be needed as a friend another. Chiefs themselves often need "political cover" when the tides of media attention turn against them. Chiefs "can't fight everybody at the same time" (Bratton and Tumin 2012, p. 261). In police governance, success for both politicians and chiefs requires mutual back-scratching.

If a disagreement can neither be ignored nor compromised, chiefs may still prevail in defending their position. They can ask for directives in writing, thus lodging responsibility with the politician for ignoring the chief's advice. As an Australian chief said:

> I would be prepared as Commissioner to accept a direction as to an operational issue but I would require it in writing so that the world could see that the responsibility had passed from the Commissioner in his independent exercise of police operations to his political master, the Minister.

The risk of this alone may cause the politician to pull back. It is especially powerful with the staff of politicians when they presume to speak with the boss' authority.

Chiefs can also appeal over the politician's head to a more senior party official, a higher level of government, or an elected council. The threat of doing so may, again, be enough to cause the politician to retreat. In so far as possible, this should be done privately. Going public is a nuclear option. In Australia, where ministers are appointed, not elected, the "nuclear option" is to take a matter to the state premier. The result usually is that either the police minister or the commissioner will have to resign, or in the case of the commissioner, face non-renewal of contract.

Educate Staff

Politicians often cultivate sources around the chief in order to obtain information about cases under investigation, targets of surveillance, newsworthy events, morale within the department, and opinions about the chief. Lower-ranking officers accept these approaches hoping to advance their careers and because it is flattering to have a personal relation with a prominent person.

Eliminating all contact with subordinate personnel is impossible, but chiefs can avoid "end runs" by requiring notification about all questions and directives from politicians and by counseling subordinates about how to handle them. A Canadian chief referred to his "famous speech" on this topic:

> Don't ever play politics. Just do your job and I'll defend you. And don't ever put up with anything that is offensive, rude, arrogant, or whatever. Tell me and I'll call off the politician.

Chiefs should also insist that politicians discipline their own staff about interactions. As an Australian chief said, "I'm not going to get on the phone and spend my time going backward and forwards with staff in the minister's office."

Finally, because chiefs cannot respond to all solicitations themselves, they should designate an officer to whom politicians can go with inquiries and get immediate attention. In short, in order to achieve political forbearance, there must be police openness.

Embrace Politics

Contrary to received wisdom, chiefs should be prepared to think and sometimes act politically. Although police chiefs must not engage in partisan policing, they need to act politically in order to obtain, in Sir Robert Peel's famous words, the consent of the public in enforcing law. This requires chiefs to inform, build alliances, and cultivate support. As one chief said:

> Politics is intrinsic to our business. Our success as police leaders, change agents, absolutely depends on our political skill set, absolutely. It's not something that we should hide from. It's not something that we should be ashamed of. It's not something that we excuse away. (Flynn 2011)

Chiefs quickly learn that conducting politics in this broad sense is time-consuming hands-on work. When William Bratton was chief in Los Angeles, he met with a variety of "constituencies"—the mayor, the Police Commission, homeless people, students, the city attorney, other department heads, the American Civil Liberties Union (ACLU), administrators of major hospitals, representatives of Business Improvement Districts (BIDs), the police union, and neighborhood crime prevention associations (Bratton and Tumin 2012, chapter 3). Such communicating must be done without stepping on the toes of politicians who court the same constituents.

Manage Appearances

Chiefs must accept the fact that news media shape the world they deal with. What the police do is news with a capital N.

The old newspaper adage is that "if it bleeds, it leads." Police stories "bleed," literally as well as figuratively. One chief remarked that over breakfast a retired chief can read the newspaper's sports page first; a serving chief reads it last.

Our interviewees were not in agreement about what is the most appropriate relationship chiefs should have with the media. Some frequently engaged with it in order "to get their message across." One Australian commissioner published a regular blog in which he discussed current policing issues and explained the police service's approach to them. Others, however, emphasized the risks of too much media exposure, particularly if it implies disagreement with the government.

In handling the media, the most basic rule is to admit mistakes, otherwise others will spread the bad news. Chiefs have one opportunity to be credible—at the beginning, not by playing catch-up. As Chuck Ramsey, the Chief in Philadelphia, observed, "Surf from the front of the wave" (pers. comm., 2013).

Chiefs also must be careful about being injected into partisanship unwittingly. For example, they should avoid responding to questions about policies advocated by politicians. This occurs particularly during election campaigns. If chiefs agree, it seems partisan; if they disagree, it generates a public quarrel. If chiefs feel compelled to speak about a policy issue, they should inform their boss in advance. At the same time, if politicians are wrong in their facts about what the police are doing or thinking, chiefs should speak up immediately.

The point is that the "optics" of their relations with politicians must always be considered. Obviously they should not endorse politicians. But they must also not allow themselves to be perceived as endorsing. Some chiefs warn against socializing with their bosses or even having their pictures taken together. For example, when Simon Overland was appointed chief commissioner of the Victoria Police in Australia, the Premier and the police minister attached his commissioner epaulets on his uniform in front of the media. The incident was forever afterward cited as "evidence" that he was too close to the Labour Government. Another commissioner felt he had been absolutely "ambushed" when he had been called up out of the audience to be included in a photograph sandwiched between the Premier and the police minister who were holding a sign that read *Victoria: Building a Law Abiding Society–Together*. This was used to launch their law-and-order policy in the forthcoming election.

The bottom line, as one chief said, was "never be mobilized" against the appearance of independence.

Take Care of Yourself

Being a chief is a stressful job, not just because of the seriousness of the work but because it requires a "whole of life commitment." "You've got to be aware of the fact that no matter what you do or where you go, it is likely to be reportable material." Therefore, in addition to learning to manage an organization, chiefs must learn to manage themselves. As an Australian chief said:

It takes a while to adjust to. If anyone's contemplating that step, my advice would be make sure that your family are committed to the task as well, because it will have a significant impact on them, and to make sure that you're prepared to deal with that day-to-day total consumption of your private life, because you cease to be a private person the day you become a commissioner.

The key, all chiefs agree, is to develop a thick skin. Chiefs must learn not to take criticism personally, even very pointed, unfair, and vindictive criticism. At the same time, they must be willing to listen to everyone, no matter how misguided or ill informed. A chief with a type A personality—always wanting to dominate—is in for trouble. People must be allowed to push back against the police publicly; they must be allowed to vent. This applies as well to people within the police organization, in particular representatives of police unions and associations. This does not mean that chiefs should never reply, even forcefully and directly. It means that they should wait until critical perspectives have been voiced and, hopefully, people are ready to listen.

Finally, but most important of all, in order to live up to their moral and legal obligations, chiefs must be prepared to resign. From day one, chiefs should be prepared to resign when they recognize that fighting is futile and acquiescence unacceptable. In effect, they must be prepared to forfeit the job they wanted in order to defend the principle of independence. The art of being a chief requires being able to make the threat of resigning credible without at the same time being unreasonable.

Conclusion

At the risk of oversimplification, the advice that chiefs give for managing the politics of their job can be boiled down to five "Big Don'ts":

1. Don't begin with a compromise.
2. Don't surprise the boss.
3. Don't monopolize credit.
4. Don't disown responsibility for mistakes.
5. Don't put ambition above principle.

This advice should be seen as "tough love" from people who have been there. It is advice that most chiefs wish they had been given before they became a top-cop (Bouza 1990; Gates and Shah 1992; Murphy and Plate 1977). All the chiefs we spoke to, regardless of country, remarked at how unprepared they were for managing the political dimension of the top job.

> If you think about it, when you become a police chief, most of the time it is the first time that you've worked for somebody who hasn't been in law enforcement, who doesn't share the same values, the same experiences, the same thing that you do, and all of a sudden you are in this different environment and not everybody does it well. (Melekian 2011)

The best training for the job comes from being a chief. The second-time-around is much easier than the first. Even being a top deputy is not preparation enough because subordinate staff "manage down," enforcing the rule-bound world of the police organization. Chiefs "manage up," with people entirely outside the chain of command, where the rules are unclear and must be negotiated with different interest groups on a daily basis (Wexler, pers. comm., 2013).

The lack of training for top managers is not unique to the police. It afflicts businesses as well as universities. Just as few people join the police with the aspiration of becoming chief, faculty members rarely go into teaching with the objective of becoming college presidents. Faculty, business leaders, and police find, surprisingly, that promotion to senior managerial positions is possible, interesting, and, perhaps, important to the success of their institutions. But formal training in management is rare at any stage of their careers. They learn about governance, external relations, and "outreach" almost exclusively through experience. If they are very lucky, they may find an experienced mentor who can provide timely advice.

References

Bouza, A. V. 1990. *The Police Mystique: An Insider's Look at Cops, Crime, and the Criminal Justice System.* New York: Plenum Press.

Bratton, W. J., and P. Knobler. 1998. *Turnaround: How America's Top Cop Reversed the Crime Epidemic.* New York: Random House.

———, and Z. Tumin. 2012. *Collaborate or Perish! Reaching Across Boundaries in a Networked World.* New York: Crown Business.

Das, D. K., and O. Marenin. 2009. *Trends in Policing: Interviews with Police Leaders across the Globe.* Boca Raton, FL: CRC Press.

Flynn, E. 2011. By Permission at the Second Executive Session on Police and Public Safety, Harvard University, November 4th.

Gates, D. F., and D. K. Shah. 1992. *Chief: My Life in the LAPD.* New York: Bantam Books.

Melekian, B. 2011. By permission at the Second Executive Session on Police and Public Safety, Harvard University, November 4th.

Murphy, P. V., and T. Plate. 1977. *Commissioner: A View from the Top of American Law Enforcement.* New York: Simon and Schuster.

Part III

Rethinking Police Governance

7

Why Governance Fails

Politicians make suggestions, direct or subtle, to police chiefs in all democratic countries. Because most are negotiated out of public sight and some are simply ignored, it is difficult to determine differences in the frequency of "suggestions" among our countries, even with the help of interviews. There is, however, a distinguishable pattern in the frequency of unresolvable disputes about the respective authority of politicians and chiefs. This emerges from our interviews with chiefs and from public accounts in the media, official inquiries, and court cases. We found that chiefs are less vulnerable to political pressure in Canada, New Zealand, and Old Britain; most vulnerable in India and the United States (see chapter 5). Australia occupies an intermediate position. Similarly, the issue of police accountability is most settled in Old Britain; reasonably settled in Australia, Canada, and New Zealand; and unsettled in India and the United States. In New Britain both directiveness and accountability issues are in transition.

Assuming this pattern is correct, what accounts for it? Why are police more vulnerable to direction in one country than another? Why is police accountability more settled in one country than another?

Explanatory Factors

The factors we will discuss to explain the differences among our countries in observable disagreements are not based on a technically scientific comparison. The sample of countries is too small for that. The explanations we present should be considered plausible hypotheses drawing on diverse sources of information and analysis. They fall into the following categories:

- Structures of police governance
- Traditions of governance
- Social structure
- Police agency characteristics
- Nature of police work
- Orientations to the job
- Personalities

It may puzzle readers that variations in reported crime rates, which are substantial, do not appear to be related to the frequency of disputes concerning respective roles between politicians and chiefs. One would think that they would cause politicians to interfere more. The fact is that none of our interviewees suggested that changes in crime rates influenced this relationship. Furthermore, reported crime data are so unreliable internationally that statistical analysis of an association between them and the role behavior of politicians and chiefs would be highly suspect. Increase in reported crime rates are certainly an important topic of conversation between chiefs and supervising politicians, but there is no evidence that they cause breakdowns in their relationship.

Structures of Governance

Given the small size of our sample, we are unable to test whether some of the general differences in governmental structures affect the success of police governance, such as parliamentary/presidential systems, federated/centralized government, and Common/Civil law. All six countries are solidly democratic; Australia, Canada, India, and the United States are federal systems; New Zealand and Britain are centralized, although Britain to a lesser extent and not with respect to police governance in either Old or New Britain. All but one have parliamentary political systems. All have Common Law legal traditions.

Looking more narrowly at institutions of police governance, it is useful to distinguish between ad hoc and general political directiveness. This distinction is implicit in the separation of policy from operational directives. Policy directives are general guidelines for police activity; operational directives apply to actions police should take in specific situations. The main finding from our interviews with police chiefs is that specific, or ad hoc, directiveness is least in countries that have created appointed boards serving as buffers between chiefs and politicians. Ad hoc directiveness is greatest where chiefs are appointed by and work directly with elected politicians.

The demand for and acceptance of the need for operational accountability has expanded in all six countries. General directiveness that is, over policy, has also expanded in all the countries of our sample. So has operational accountability. Ad hoc directiveness has diminished in four of our countries but not in India and the United States.

We also found an unexpected association between directiveness and accountability. Larger amounts of directiveness do not seem to contribute to greater satisfaction about accountability. Quite the contrary. Although politicians may be satisfied, the public in countries with high directiveness tends to be unhappy about accountability. Conversely, the public in countries with less directiveness tends to be more satisfied about accountability. Simply put, the goal of achieving acceptable accountability is not served by increased political directiveness. Increased directiveness is acceptable, it would seem, if it is accompanied by increased accountability not of the police but the politicians themselves. The public needs to be assured that political directiveness is not misused.

Traditions of Governance

Not surprisingly there are fewer disputes about police governance in countries where visible ad hoc direction of the police by politicians is anathema. If politicians understand that public opinion is not on their side, the police can invoke operational independence with greater impunity. Values can shape behavior independently of formal governance structures. By rallying public opinion, slogans like "operational independence" can protect police from directive interference.

Traditions, however, can change. Non-interference in operational matters can wax and wane as a virtue. It has waned in Australia and New Zealand in the last thirty years. The zeitgeist has changed over time in the United States too. Sam Walker describes the "truly kaleidoscopic variety of forms" of police governance in the last half of the nineteenth century (Walker 1977, 26). The creation of Police Commissions to protect police from partisan direction was very popular then but fell out of favor until the late twentieth century. The city of Cincinnati, Ohio, for example, had ten major changes in governance between 1859 and 1910. Two civilian complaint review boards in New York City and Philadelphia were abolished in the 1960s (Walker 1977). A referendum to create direct community control through neighborhood boards was rejected in Berkeley, California, at the same time. In sum, the United States has experimented with police governance continually but has failed to develop, except in a patchwork way, an alternative to direct political oversight.

Relating institutions of police governance to traditions of government can be tricky. It has been suggested, for example, that Americans have always been more distrustful of government than the British (Fosdick 1915; Miller 1977; Richardson 1974; Smith 1949). Americans eternally tinker with the machinery of government, searching for ways to limit power, especially executive power, while the British trust their politicians and professional staff to do the right thing without so many checks and balances. The British have greater tolerance than Americans for entrusting government to an "establishment" of people. If this is true, then the British ought to be more tolerant of political direction, Americans less. One would expect the United States to have appointed boards limiting partisanship in police and holding the police to account. Paradoxically, until the Police Reform and Social Responsibility Act of 2011, it was the British and Canadians who had developed local mediating Police Authorities, while Americans preferred direct political supervision, modified only by the development of city managers.

India is particularly paradoxical in this respect. Considering its oppressive colonial history, one would think that upon gaining independence (1947), they would have thrown out the colonial *Police Act* enacted in 1861. But as one former police commissioner has written (Dhillon 2005, 566–67):

A flurry of activity in the first few decades after independence, directed at conducting an in-depth examination of the structure and functional modes of police in India, failed to bring about even an iota of change.

Dhillon's explanation is that the colonial Police Act served the purposes of a new government faced with major problems of law-and-order. Order took precedence over reform. In any case, by the late 1960s and early 1970s, state-based politicians had taken direct control and did not want to give it up (Dhillon 2005; Verma 2000, 2011).

Social Structure

The contentiousness of the relationship between politicians and police seems to be related to the diversity of the population. In multiethnic and multiracial populations, politicians are more likely to use the police to favor their constituencies. If an ethnic group has been disadvantaged historically, its political representatives will strive to ensure equality in the application of law as well as in hiring and promoting within the police. This would explain why politicians in the United States and India are more directive than elsewhere. They fear to relinquish control.

In India, there may be another reason why heterogeneity encourages directiveness. Indians distrust government generally, not only the police but the judiciary and appointed, regulatory bureaucrats. Indians may deplore political intervention in policing, but they seem to have greater faith in "their" politicians than the impersonal system. Politicians know this, and believe that responding to pleas for help, or at least seeming to, is regarded as essential for popularity.

Greater homogeneity may explain why police-governance traditions in Australia and New Zealand are more like that of Old Britain and less like that of the United States or India. It does not apply to Canada, however, which is also socially diverse but today enjoys comparatively harmonious police–political relations mediated by Police Boards. The explanation for the popularity of Police Boards in Canada may be that they are accepted as part of "good government," which is stipulated along with "peace" and "order" in its 1867 constitution. The US constitution, as many have pointed out, does not guarantee good government, but life, liberty, and pursuit of happiness. Contrary to Canada, the constitution of the United States does not valorize government; it valorizes liberty.

The problem with this explanation for the creation of independent, nonpolitical buffers between police and politicians, although it fits the facts in our sample, is paradoxical. Why would a diverse population not be more inclined to support the development of depoliticizing institutions than less diverse ones? If people do not fear partisanship in policing, as in India and the United States, why would they adopt mediated police governance? Clearly, the impact of social diversity needs more analysis.

Police Agency Characteristics

Many observers as well as police chiefs believe that the size of the police jurisdiction makes a difference in the degree of political interference. In smaller jurisdictions relations between police and politicians are cozier because they are more likely to know one another personally. A US chief noted that the politicians and police officers where he had recently been hired wore the same high-school graduation ring. Similarly, the media in smaller jurisdictions may be less distrustful of political direction due to greater personal familiarity.

The chiefs we interviewed did not think that geographical location within a country made a difference to directiveness or accountability, except in Canada and the United States. Canadian and US chiefs, as well as scholars, generally believe that political interference across government is greater in the east due to its legacy of powerful, entrenched political machines than in the west, which instituted good government reforms later in history. The supervision of police by city managers, for example, rather than mayors and city councils is more common in the west than the east.

Chiefs in all countries thought that being appointed from inside made them more vulnerable to political direction than being appointed from other agencies or other countries. Insiders bring local connectedness that obligates them in ways that do not apply to outsiders.

The chiefs in our sample also generally agreed that fixed-term contracts lessen political leverage compared with appointments "at pleasure." Fixed-term contracts, however, increase leverage compared with tenured appointments in which incumbents can only be terminated "for cause." Knowing that the opportunity for a change is looming, a chief keen to be re-appointed might become more accommodating to political demands. Vulnerability to influence is to some extent a constant in policing regardless of the terms of appointment. But because "at pleasure" contracts are most common in the United States and India, US and Indian police chiefs feel more vulnerable to ad hoc political directiveness.

Nature of Police Work

Politicians pay closer attention to certain kinds of police work than to others. The more serious security issues become, the more likely it is for politicians to become involved. The clearest example is the rising importance of terrorism. Not only is local interest likely to rise, but it is more likely for national levels of government to become involved. This is more likely in countries with centralized control over police, such as Britain and New Zealand. It also occurs in countries with decentralized police, such as the United States and India, when co-ordination among levels of government becomes critically important.

There may be a general principle here: as police responsibilities are extended from threats to individuals to threats to society as a whole, policing becomes more sensitive politically. By extension, when the police mandate broadens from deterrent law enforcement to proactive crime prevention, political directiveness becomes more likely.

Orientations to the Job

It is important to distinguish the orientations that politicians and chiefs bring into their jobs from aspects of their personalities. Orientations are matters of choice; they can be negotiated. Personalities, however, are givens; they may be worked around but are unlikely to change. The orientations that are most likely to challenge distributions of authority are, respectively:

(1) For politicians
   • Reformist/status quo
   • Role assertive/accommodating
(2) For police
   • Reformist/status quo
   • Role defensive/accommodating

The key orientation that directly affects directiveness is the ambitiousness of the respective protagonists. If politicians are ambitious, perhaps viewing their position as a stepping stone to greater things, they are more likely to want to demonstrate their managerial competence and especially to protect their reputations. They are also more likely to be directive if they are reformist in orientation, coming to the job with an agenda to implement. If chiefs, on the other hand, are ambitious or reformist, they are likely to be more resentful of interference and hence defensive in the face of perceived political pressure or resistance. If they are content, however, simply to "tend the store," they will be more likely to "go along to get along." The accidental pairings of respective orientations are crucial. An overweening politician with a defensive chief is the most troublesome. Any other combination of assertion and nonassertion of prerogatives is compatible as far as governance is concerned.

Personalities

Police chiefs as well as police scholars believe that personalities can be crucial. As an Australian chief said, "Your difficulties generally arise out of quirky personalities and lack of capability in the ministers." The particular features of personality that trouble governance are, respectively:

(1) For politicians
- Dogmatic/open-minded
- Controlling/delegating
- Insecure/confident
- Self-centered/empathetic

(2) For chiefs
- Dogmatic/open-minded
- Anxious/confident

Some of these aspects of personality create difficulties when either player holds them. Others become difficult when they are mismatched with the other. As an Australian chief said of police ministers, "the ones who know the ropes don't have to be hands-on, the ones who don't know, they're more inclined to be hands-on." The bottom line is that personalities often matter more than formal arrangements. Personal dynamics can upset any structural apple cart.

Conclusion

Developing hypotheses about factors that explain differences in the success of police governance is admittedly difficult with so small a sample. The following are the most plausible influencing factors that appear to be associated with more harmonious police governance:

- Mediating police boards
- Strong traditions of operational independence
- Positive public orientations to government
- Homogeneous populations
- Large police forces
- Appointment of chiefs from outside the agency
- Fixed-term renewable contracts for police chiefs
- Narrowly focused, reactive police work
- Unambitious politicians and chiefs
- Confident and open personalities

Are these factors informative for observers in democratic countries or should they be attributed to characteristics of our six-country sample? In other words, should they be taken seriously for improving democratic police governance when countries have so many differences? This issue was raised at the end of chapter 4. We believe that tentative though these hypotheses are, they are informative because most of them are independent of the most prominent contextual differences— physical, structural, governmental—with the sole exception of social diversity. In other words, limiting the sample to democracies does not overwhelm what can be learned about the contextual correlates of success in police governance. If an international comparison included non-democratic countries this would not be true. If the directiveness of government generally, not just of the police, were overwhelming, then other differences in context might not plausibly be associated. In sum, if one lives in a democratic country, it is worthwhile to learn, at least speculate, about the effect of contextual differences on police governance from our sample.

The list of contextual factors explaining differences in the success of police governance suggests what can and cannot be done to improve a country's record. The possibilities for planned reform on this list are limited. Only three can be reliably manipulated by reformist-minded governments, namely, creating mediating institutions such as Police Boards, appointing chiefs from other forces, and appointing chiefs for renewable fixed-terms.

Even the appointment of chiefs from outside the agency and fixed-term contracts may not be conducive to the success of the relationship depending on circumstances. In the case of external appointments, success will depend on how well the new chief adapts to and accommodates established traditions of the jurisdiction to which he or she has come. Some Australian states have had some bad experiences in this respect when they have "imported" new commissioners from Britain or from other Australian states, and in one case from neighboring New Zealand.

As far as the introduction of fixed-term contracts is concerned, it depends on what they have replaced. When they replace appointments "at pleasure" they may have a beneficial effect on police chief–political supervisor relationships because they place the two parties on a more even footing in negotiating. When they replace tenured appointments that can only be terminated "for (specified) cause," however, they are likely to have the opposite effect. In this case, chiefs know that if they don't "toe the line," their contracts may simply not be renewed.

Three other contextual factors would be difficult to change at all, at least in the short term—generalized distrust of government, diversity of population, and creating larger police forces. The size of police jurisdictions can be changed in principle, but history shows that it is very difficult politically (Bayley 1975). Britain and Canada are the only counties in the sample that have substantially changed the size of jurisdictions over time.[1] Both have replaced some small local forces with larger regional ones. Australia and India have based policing on their states from independence. New Zealand has always had centralized police. The United States built police up from localities since its founding, giving them the privileged place they still retain.

The final three factors—character of police work and the job orientations and personalities of politicians and chiefs—are wild cards, neither manipulable nor predictable. Given our inability to predict future threats to public safety, it is impossible to foresee the scope of police work. Old threats may recede, new ones will emerge. Public needs and public fears will drive the police agenda, which in turn will raise new challenges to governance. Similarly, reliably vetting politicians and chiefs for their orientations and personalities is very difficult. The tools to do so are questionable and politics is likely in any case to be more influential in making appointments than science.

This roster of factors explaining the success of police governance should be taken seriously in a reform agenda in democratic countries. Having a democratic national government or democratic traditions are not enough. Other factors should be taken into account.

Note

1.   Scotland recently changed from eight regional services to one national service.

References

Bayley, D. H. 1975. "The Police and Political Development in Europe." In *The Formation of National States in Europe*, edited by C. Tilley, Chap. 5, 328–455. Princeton, NJ: Princeton University Press.

Dhillon, K. 2005. *Police and Politics in India: Colonial Concepts, Democratic Compulsions: Indian Police 1947-2002*. New Delhi: Manohar Publishers.

Fosdick, R. B. 1915. *European Police Systems*. New York: Century Company.

Miller, W. R. 1977. *Cops and Bobbies: Police Authority in New York and London, 1830-1870*. Chicago, IL: University of Chicago Press.

Richardson, J. F. 1974. *Urban Police in the United States*. New York: Oxford University Press.

Smith, B. 1949. *Police Systems in the United States*. New York: Harper and Row.

Verma, A. 2000. "Politicisation of the police in India: Where lies the blame?" *Indian Police Journal* 47(4): 19–37.

———. 2011. *The New Khaki: The Evolving Nature of Police in India*. Boca Raton, FL: CRC Press.

Walker, Samuel. 1977. *A Critical History of Police Reform: The Emergence of Professionalism*. New York: Lexington Books.

8

The Changing Contexts of Governance

Police governance in democracies does not take place in a vacuum, but within broader conceptions and expectations of what democratic governance means and requires, and how it should be achieved. So achieving successful democratic police governance is not just about reducing conflicts between chiefs and their political supervisors, although of course that is important. While a focus on disputes shows the dynamics of the relationship as it is experienced by chiefs and to a lesser extent by politicians, it oversimplifies what is going on. It does so because it concentrates on failures of governance, either from too much directiveness or too little accountability. This misses the complexity of the give-and-take that goes on constantly between politicians and cops and the range of influences bearing on police that might be considered "political."

To be considered "successful" in a twenty-first century democracy, police governance must reflect and embody contemporary views of what democratic governance requires and how it should be accomplished. Views about this have changed significantly in most of our six countries during the last forty years, albeit to different extents and at different paces. So we need to consider what appear to be the most significant developments in this respect, and consider what implications they have had for views of what is required for good police governance in general and appropriate chief-political supervisor relationships in particular.

We begin by noting the shift that has taken place in four of our countries from the long-held view that police governance is *sui generis*—requiring different principles from those which apply to other departments and agencies of governance—to the view that it should generally reflect the same principles as are applied in all other areas of government. We then review five developments which, in at least four of our six countries, have accounted for this shift, and in each case describe the specific impact that these developments have had on understandings of police governance generally and of the police chief–political supervisor relationship in particular.

Historically police governance has been thought of in our six countries as requiring a unique degree of independence from political direction compared with other governmental activities, such as education and health, with accountability primarily to the law rather than politicians. This was justified in terms of a requirement to ensure that the police were not deployed by governments for partisan political purposes to suppress opposition and dissent, and that their main role was the enforcement of law. Their role was viewed as part of the criminal justice system, therefore being quasi-judicial. This view persists in Civil Law countries, such as Spain and France, where police not only initiate the application of law but investigate and to some extent adjudicate under judicial supervision. The rationale is to ensure that investigations are immune from political direction (Hodgson 2005).

In Common Law countries, such as our six countries, the perceived need for political independence was initially achieved by putting the police under the supervision of magistrates rather than politicians. The famous Bow Street Runners, for instance, were established and governed by the Bow Street Magistrates (the Fielding brothers), not by politicians, and the London Metropolitan Police, when it was established in 1829, was governed by two justices of the peace, albeit with some supervision by the Home Secretary. During the nineteenth and early twentieth centuries, however, responsibility for governing the police was gradually transferred from magistrates to elected politicians, either local or national. As we explained in chapter 3, in order to ensure that they would not become "government police" and deployed for partisan purposes, a doctrine of "police independence" was gradually developed, whereby their so-called "quasi-judicial" law enforcement responsibilities were considered not to be subject to political direction and, in some formulations of this doctrine (notably Lord Denning's in the *Blackburn* case), the police were also not considered to be politically accountable for their exercise of these functions, but rather were deemed to be accountable "to the law and to the law alone." This view of police governance has persisted in four of our six countries (Australia, Britain, Canada, and New Zealand) to this day.

Within this conception, police governance continued to be viewed as *sui generis* and the central issue in police governance came to be usually described as balancing political oversight and police independence. Politicians felt constrained to defer to "police independence," and police chiefs, supported by the courts, insisted that they should enjoy wide political independence in running their police forces.

In the United States, this pursuit of independence was undertaken in a different way, through a campaign by some leading chiefs, such as August Vollmer in Berkeley and O.W. Wilson in Chicago, to "professionalize" the police, and have police chiefs recognized as professionals who were entitled to a high degree of autonomy in running their police forces (Fogelson 1977). To some extent, but far less success-fully, this has also been an aspiration of police chiefs in India.

Many of our interviewees in Australia, Britain, New Zealand, and to a lesser degree Canada, have told us that beginning in the 1970s attitudes toward police governance began to change. Specifically, they have told us that during the last four decades police governance, and their relationships with their political supervisors, have become noticeably more "political" or "politicized." The recent change in New Britain from local Police Authorities to locally elected Police and Crime Commissioners, for instance, was strongly opposed by many senior police leaders there on the ground that it would "politicize" policing and the police and undermine their independence (Shaw 2013).

While lip service is still paid to police independence with respect to law enforcement in "individual cases," governments began to assume a much more proactive role in governing the police, and police came more and more to be regarded as subject to the same government supervision and political accountability as other government departments. That is, acceptance of the view that police governance was unique began to steadily decline; government direction of the police expanded to more and more aspects of their functions, and they were held politically accountable for all of their activities. The idea that police are not politically accountable for any of their "law enforcement" activities, was rejected. It was only accepted that police should not be politically accountable with respect to individual criminal investigations and other police operations while they are still in progress.

The movement from thinking that the police are *sui generis* among governmental agencies allows changes in the contexts of policing to have greater impact on the relations between politicians and police executives. Police are no longer seen as immune from changes in their environment.

We believe that five changes in the context of police governance have been particularly influential, although not to the same degree in all six countries of our sample.

1. Changing conceptions of democracy and the kind of governance required.
2. Changing attitudes toward the respective roles of government and civil society, sometimes referred to as "neoliberalism."
3. A public service reform movement, often called "New Public Management."
4. Changing attitudes toward "professionalism."
5. The development of new communication and surveillance technologies.

Changing Conceptions of Democracy

Beginning in the 1960s, increasing calls for more open government, enhanced government accountability, greater access to information, and more "participatory" democracy began to emerge in almost every Western democracy (Bohman 1996; Pateman 1970). The idea of representative democracy in which key government decisions were made in private with public input only at the discretion of the government in power, and in which the only serious opportunity for citizen influence over governance was at election time was increasingly rejected in favor of a view of governance as a "co-production" between the governors and the governed. To facilitate greater public input into government decisions, public consultations, "town hall meetings," freedom of information legislation, frequent open parliamentary hearings and reviews of government policies and decisions, and interviews and debates with politicians in public affairs programs on radio and television, became normal and expected modes of democratic governance (Dahl 1989). All areas of government, including the police and other criminal justice agencies, were subject to these new expectations of democratic governance (Stenning 1995).

The impact of this transformation of democratic governance on police governance has been dramatic in those countries in which it has occurred. Its impact has been of four kinds, which we consider in turn:

- Changing practices of police-governing authorities
- Establishment of new oversight institutions
- New community and neighborhood organizations
- New approaches to policing and citizen involvement

Changing Practices of Police-governing Authorities

Meetings of police-governing authorities that were previously closed to the public were opened to public attendance and their agendas were advertised in advance. In many cases public hearings were held at which policing priorities, the police budget, and other significant matters of police policy were opened up for public submissions and discussion, and community concerns about particular police activities or priorities could be publicly aired. Police-governing authorities' offices were moved out of police headquarters into buildings that were more publicly accessible and implied some visible independence from the police themselves. The governing authorities began to "reach out" to their communities by holding some of their meetings in community venues such as community halls and schools. Throughout the 1970s and beyond, police governance and interactions between police chiefs and their political supervisors were transformed from being activities that had previously taken place behind closed doors in access-controlled police and government buildings, to interactions which were conducted in public and subject to public scrutiny, input, and questioning.

New Oversight Institutions

The impact of these new understandings and expectations of democratic governance was not confined to the practices of traditional police-governing authorities. An array of new oversight institutions were created during this period. Although there were precursor oversight agencies for the police in Britain, Canada, and the United States in the nineteenth century, oversight has expanded dramatically since the 1960s to a raft of new agencies. Heretofore the formal mechanisms of oversight were legislatures, elected executives, judges, and governmental legal officers. This is still largely true in India but not elsewhere.

In the other five countries a wide range of new oversight institutions have been introduced. For example, in Britain an Independent Police Complaints Commission was established in 1984, and similar institutions have been established in most of our other five countries. Chief constables in Britain may now report to as many as thirty distinct agencies, each with a specialized oversight remit (Peter Neyroud, pers. comm., August 2014; Hugh Orde, pers. comm., July 2014). A partial list includes the Health and Safety Executive, the Equality and Human Rights Commission, the Office of the Surveillance Commissioners, and the Information Commissioner. British law also explicitly recognizes international oversight by the European Court of Human Rights under the Helsinki Declaration (1948). Police services in Britain are regularly subject to audits by the Audit Commission and inspections by Her Majesty's Inspector of Constabulary whose reports are published.

In the United States it is now considered the mark of a progressive police department to be audited by the Commission for Accreditation of Law Enforcement Agencies (CALEA), founded in 1979. Police departments that volunteer for accreditation must meet close to five hundred stipulated standards (Gary Cordner, commissioner, private communication, 24 July 14). Since the late 1980s civilian review boards have been created in over one hundred jurisdictions (Walker 2005). Although their powers as well as their composition vary enormously, they were created primarily to receive complaints about misbehavior by police officers and to oversee, and in some cases conduct, investigations. Finally, policing in the United States has historically been conducted under State or local authorization. Since 1997, however, the federal government has inserted another layer of oversight, undertaking over fifty investigations of police compliance with civil rights statutes. If violations are found, the Department of Justice can require police departments to agree to specified reforms overseen by appointed monitors under judicial supervision. There have been over twenty of these consent decrees. The monitoring process can last for as long as a decade and impose appreciable costs in terms of time, and resources.

New Community and Neighborhood Organizations

In all six countries, community- or neighborhood-based organizations have been created to advise the police and assist in crime prevention. Because experience has shown that they require police involvement in order to remain active (Skogan and Frydel 2004), police departments commonly assign personnel to assist them. Maintaining suitable contact takes considerable time by officers of all ranks, including chiefs.

Co-ordination of activities within and among levels of government has also become more complex. Proactive crime prevention, especially under the methodology of problem-oriented policing, requires a whole-of-government approach involving departments of education, recreation, sanitation, transportation, traffic engineering, and public health. Furthermore, many of the crimes that the public is concerned about, such as narcotics and sex trafficking, terrorism, pornography, commercial fraud, and cybercrime, are no longer exclusively local. They require the co-ordination of intelligence gathering and enforcement operations among jurisdictions up and down levels of government, as well as with private security agencies.

New Approaches to Policing and Citizen Involvement

It is not just police governance and oversight institutions that have been impacted by changed understandings and expectations of democracy. The very business of policing has also been transformed. Probably the best known manifestation of this has been the "community-based policing" movement, which involves consultation with communities with respect to policing priorities, complaints about policing, and virtually any other matter that members of the community want to be heard about. This has given opportunities for a myriad of politically powerful constituencies that police cannot afford to ignore. Their number has grown exponentially. They include crime victims, schools, people with mental illness, elderly persons, business associations, minority groups, religious institutions, hospitals, new immigrants, and gays and lesbians. One big-city US chief estimated that not more than 20 percent of his decisions were made by him without consultation outside the department (Batts, pers. Comm., November 4, 2011).

There are two reasons for this growth. First, groups representing these interests have become increasingly sophisticated in articulating demands and mobilizing support, and second, the police themselves have encouraged involvement of communities in crime control. Proactive crime prevention has become a recognized specialization within the police, separate from patrolling and criminal investigation. Police specialists now provide advice about minimizing risks to businesses and homeowners, publish pamphlets about self-protection, organize self-defense groups, such as Neighborhood Watch, and collaborate with city planners and architects.

Public opinion impinges on police in other ways as well. It comes through formal surveys of satisfaction/suspicion of the police, which are duly reported in the media. Investigative reports are frequently published about police activities by a host of non-governmental organizations, such as Amnesty International, Human Rights Watch, and the American Civil Liberties Union (ACLU). In many cities advocacy groups apply to the police for permission to demonstrate in public. Police negotiate with them, sometimes at great length, about timing, use of sidewalks, obstruction of traffic, and their own protection. People in favor of a cause criticize the police for being too restrictive; people against it criticize the police for being too tolerant. Regardless of what they do, the police appear to somebody to have been partisan.

Because of the diffusion of oversight, modern police feel that they live in an echo chamber. Nothing can be assumed to be out of sight, exposure reverberates loud and long. From the police point of view, the "political" is now much wider than their relationship with a few elected officials. They feel they need to cultivate their own political base that can be rallied when crises arise (Bratton 2012; Gates 1992). As Robert Mark, commissioner of the London Metropolitan Police, wrote:

> It did not take me long to appreciate that the only way to win was to go over the heads of politicians and the civil service and appeal to public opinion in moderate and persuasive terms, backed up by irrefutable statistical evidence. (Mark 1978, 129)

Cultivating public opinion, another chief said, was her "trump card" in dealing with the political chain of command. As sensible as this advice sounds, it must be done with great care. Politicians see it as an invasion of their territory, a direct threat to their own representative prerogatives. Ironically, police chiefs are redefining traditional notions of interference, oversight, and professionalism, not in order to protect themselves from politics but to excuse their own participation in it.

But that is not easy. This pressure for community engagement has put police chiefs in the public spotlight in a way that politicians are used to, but most police chiefs are not. As one Australian police commissioner put it:

> The role of the Commissioner has become much more public, much more political. I think what is frequently underestimated is that public nature of the Commissioner's role, the fact that it is in every sense a whole of life commitment. You are likely to be scrutinised 24 hours a day. You've got to be aware of the fact that no matter what you do or where you go, it is likely to be reportable material. It is a commitment that affects the whole of the family and not just yourself, and can impact very specifically, in a media and a public sense, on your family, on your wife and your children, in a way that can be destructive and can be very difficult. And I think, sadly, the role of the commissioner has changed to the extent where it is going to become increasingly difficult to get good men to put up their hands to do it.

Inadvertently stealing the limelight from your political supervisor has become a challenge for some popular police chiefs.

All of these developments have expanded dramatically what democratic police governance is now understood to entail, and who both police chiefs and political supervisors must pay attention to in the process. The idea that police governance can be enacted between a police chief and his or her supervisor in private has disappeared, as has the notion that a broad conception of police independence from political "interference" is still acceptable. Indeed, the very ideas of "police independence" and associated "improper political interference" have had to be revised and re-negotiated in light of the greatly increased demands for, and expectations of, openness and accountability, both of political supervisors and of police chiefs. Police chiefs who cling to outdated notions of their immunity from political direction and accountability soon find themselves in trouble. Political supervisors feel the need to be increasingly involved in, or at least kept constantly informed about, matters of police administration and policy in order to meet the demands on themselves for public and parliamentary accountability. This is what explains the view which so many of our interviewees have expressed, sometimes in a tone of exasperation or resignation, that during recent decades policing and the job of police chiefs have become increasingly "politicized."

These different conceptions of democracy and the kind of governance it requires continue to evolve as theorists put forward proposals to make democracy more inclusive, and more "deliberative," and explore new ways to increase civil society engagement in democratic governance (Dryzek 2000). To what extent they presage future changes in attitudes and practices of democracy remains to be seen.

Changing Attitudes toward the Roles of Government and Civil Society

Referred to as "Neoliberalism," this is a philosophy of government according to which governments should intervene in citizens' lives no more than is necessary to ensure order and facilitate a free market economy (Larner 1997; Larner and Walters 2000). Governments should be "lean" and efficient and should "get out of the way" so that citizens and business can pursue their interests unhampered by unnecessary bureaucracy and government intervention in their affairs. It was popularized by a book by Americans David Osborne and Ted Gaebler, entitled *Reinventing Government: How the Entrepreneurial Spirit is Transforming the Public Sector* (1992),[1] and became particularly well known for its metaphor that governments should "steer but not row," that is, take responsibility for seeing that services are provided but not provide them themselves. Furthermore, governments should introduce market principles into the governance of monopolistic government enterprises. The philosophy, however, had already been promoted in the United States and Britain well before Osborne and Gaebler published their book, and had been particularly associated with the Reagan administration in the United States and the Thatcher government in the Britain (Jones 2012). Its impact was to encourage radical "downsizing" of the public service, and "outsourcing" or "devolving" the provision of former government services to the private sector or to civil society. Other terms that were used to describe the impacts of this governance philosophy were that the state would be "hollowed out" and that local communities and the citizenry would be "responsibilized." Pursuing this philosophy, governments challenged agencies to justify their continued existence or face drastic cuts to their staff and budgets, even complete abolition.

At first, the police remained relatively immune to these impacts as they were perceived to be an essential government service. But this immunity did not last. It was not long before the government in Britain was insisting that the police look for ways to outsource traditional police support functions such as procurement, transport of prisoners, and fleet maintenance, or face cuts. For example, the Lincolnshire police outsourced almost all its "organizational services" to a private security company for a budget saving of almost 18 percent. This had to be negotiated with and approved by the new Lincolnshire Police and Crime Commissioner (G4S 2013).

In Britain, neoliberalism has been a progressive trend, culminating most recently in the Cameron government's requirement for 20 percent or more budget cuts across the public service, including the police service, over a period of three years. This has involved a greatly increased government intervention into matters of police administration, mainly through the Audit Commission and Her Majesty's Inspector of Constabulary. Police chiefs have had to start finding ways to achieve these cuts without compromising frontline police services to the public. Chief constables have thus become major corporate managers, and the chief-political supervisor relationship more like a CEO-Chairman of the board relationship than the traditional relationship defined by notions of "police independence."

More generally, the privatization and pluralization of policing provision has meant that what used to be police policy has become *policing* policy, in which the public police services have become but one, albeit still dominant, player. Recognizing this trend, the 1999 report of the Patten Inquiry into policing in Northern Ireland recommended that a Policing Board be established to govern policing in the province, and that it should have a policing, rather than a police, budget and allocate this budget between public, private, and community organizations which would bid for shares of it. Under this scheme, the Chief Constable of the Police Service of Northern Ireland would have been one of several organizations submitting bids to his political supervisors for its share of the budget. The report's recommendation for a Policing Board was adopted, but the budget proposal was not. But it may foreshadow a future development in police-political supervisor relationships.

Public Service Reform

While neoliberalism seems to have had its greatest impact on police governance in Britain out of our six countries, one of the other developments arising from it is what has come to be known as "New Public Management," which has had its greatest impact on police governance in Australia and New Zealand among our six countries. There is some disagreement as to which country pioneered the New Public Management

(NPM) approach to public service management, but it has often been associated with the Lange Labour Government in New Zealand, and its Finance Minister, Roger Douglas (Hood 1995; Martin 1988; Scott, Bushnell, and Sallee 1990). The basic features of the NPM are (1) government departments and agencies are treated as service providers with whom the government contracts through purchase agreements for the provision of public services, and are monitored for contract compliance; (2) heads of departments and agencies are hired on renewable fixed-term contracts, typically of three- or five-year duration, rather than as permanent appointees; and (3) public service employees, including heads of departments and agencies, are subject to regular performance reviews to ensure contract compliance.

The term "purchase agreement" is used exclusively in Australia and New Zealand. It specifies all the services that police organizations undertake to deliver to the government over a specified period time, such as crime prevention, traffic regulation, and drug enforcement. Some include key performance indicators. The police chief is accountable for the organization's delivery of the services specified in the agreement.

The introduction of NPM in New Zealand and Australia has transformed the relationship between police and their governments (Yeatman 1987). Purchase agreements have significantly expanded governments' directive authority with respect to police services, and the demands on police commissioners to account for their management of the service and their own performance. Of the three features of NPM just mentioned, our interviewees have told us that the replacement of permanent appointment by renewable fixed-term contract appointments has had the greatest impact on the chief–political supervisor relationship. Perhaps the most important implication is that governments no longer have the same need to publicly justify termination of commissioner appointments, unless they want to terminate their contracts prematurely. Police commissioner resistance to ministerial intervention has become more risky since it can easily lead to non-renewal of their contracts. This encourages ministers to be bolder and commissioners to be more compliant, or at least more diligent in seeking compromises in resolving any disagreements they may have with their ministers. Previous broad understandings of the scope and implications of "police independence" have become largely irrelevant and unacceptable in this governance environment, and this concept can now only be successfully invoked as a response to the most blatant partisan political attempts to interfere in individual law enforcement operations. Ministers know this and generally avoid such interventions.

Like purchase agreements, fixed-term contracts have enabled governments to exercise greater influence over police decisions that were previously considered to be the exclusive prerogative of police commissioners. The position descriptions under which police commissioners are appointed illustrate this. The most recent position description for the chief commissioner in Victoria, for instance, includes the following among the responsibilities of the chief commissioner:

- Provide superior leadership to ensure a commitment to service excellence and a corporate culture which supports community and Government priorities; develop corporate plans which accommodate Government requirements and provide effective reporting on performance to Government.
- Develop and implement policing strategies which are in accordance with Government priorities, including the promotion of a strong commitment by Victoria Police to community safety, family violence, counter-terrorism, road safety and crime prevention programs.
- Ensure that Victoria Police manages its resources within its overall budgetary allocation in accordance with Government policies and priorities and implement contemporary management and

information technology systems, to improve efficiency and effectiveness, and enhance productivity and overall policing outcomes for the community.

Our interviewees were not agreed about the benefits and drawbacks of these police governance arrangements. Some welcomed the more consultative, cooperative chief–political supervisor relationship that they engender. Others bemoaned the erosion of police commissioners' political independence. All agreed that things are not now as they used to be.

NPM has influenced police–government relations in some of these ways in Britain (Pollitt 1993) as well as in Australia and New Zealand. The introduction of the new local Police and Crime Commissioners may make NPM more salient to the chief–political supervisor relationship than it was in Old Britain with its multimember Police Authorities. It is too soon to tell. Although NPM has also had some traction in Canada (Aucoin 1990) and the United States (Pollitt 1993), the large number, smaller size, and more local jurisdiction of police services in those countries seems to have meant that it has had less impact. It seems to have had no discernible impact on police–government relations in India.

Changing Attitudes toward Professionalism

In the United States from about the 1920s onward, increased police autonomy and freedom from unwanted "political interference" was thought to be best pursued by a policy of police "professionalization." The idea was to establish police (or at least police leaders) as professionals who could expect a higher public status, a high degree of occupational autonomy and, like other professionals such as doctors and lawyers, a right to self-government (Larson 1979). The International Association of Chiefs of Police, which had been established as far back as 1893, provided an important platform through which to promote this agenda. One of its goals was "to encourage adherence of all police officers to high professional standards of performance and conduct" (http://www.theiacp.org/History). To this day its mission statement begins with the words "The IACP shall advance professional police services." Police officers were encouraged to enroll in universities and colleges if they sought advancement, and by the 1960s a few of the larger police services in the United States required recruits to have an undergraduate university or college degree. Police leaders also began to pursue MBA degrees and other management or business qualifications.

By the late 1960s, however, professionalism, and in particular the assumed right of professionals to govern themselves without government interference, was coming into question. Attitudes toward democratic governance were changing, including a distrust of "government by experts" and professional self-government in particular (Walker 1977).

Despite these challenges, the idea of police professionalism has certainly not disappeared (Walker 1977). In the extensive writing about police governance, "professionalism" has been used to refer to the expertise police have in the management of public safety that should not be compromised by non-experts (Sklansky 2011; Stone and Travis 2011). It is still viewed as a desirable constraint on political directiveness. Current advocates of a "new professionalism in policing" (Stone and Travis 2011), however, do not advocate it as a road to greater immunity from political oversight, but as a means to achieve greater public accountability and legitimacy. This reflects the re-definition of the "political" in police governance that we discussed earlier.

Questions have persisted as to what precisely is the expertise that politicians should defer to as professional. As with the other problematic terms like "police independence," the content of professionalism is unclear. For example, should it include strategies for preventing crime, tactics in handling public demonstrations, decisions to make arrests, protocols for interrogations, recommendations about weaponry, creation of specialized squads, and the fairness of disciplinary processes? In the last few years, the reach of "professionalism" has expanded to include "best practices," referring to actions widely accepted among police leaders as being effective in the public interest. Sometimes "best practices" have been validated by rigorous evaluation, many times not. Whether "best practices" are professional is a matter of debate.

There is an added complication about invoking "professionalism" in discussions of police governance. Having unique expertise does not mean that police can do what they want without oversight. "Professionalism" must at least accommodate responsibility. By the same token, it would seem to imply a role for the police in policy making. If "professionalism" is based on unique expertise, then it should be shared publicly when policy decisions are being made about public safety. "Professionalism" seems to entail an obligation for police to become "political" when doing so is in the public interest.

Because the content of professionalism is unclear, it too, like other problematic terms, must be negotiated on an ongoing basis. It is too ambiguous to be used to create boundaries for defining "interference" and "operational."

New Communication and Surveillance Technologies

During the last twenty-five years, the development of new communication and surveillance technologies has transformed governance in all of our six countries, albeit more dramatically and earlier in some than in others. These new technologies include the internet and associated "social media," mobile phones with photographic and video capabilities, as well as internet access, closed-circuit television (CCTV), and "Big Data" computational capacities. Between them they have enhanced communication between police, police-governing authorities, and the citizenry, as well as public accountability of policing.

Social media, abetted by ubiquitous phone cameras, have emerged as new accountability mechanisms. Through platforms like U-Tube, Facebook, and Twitter, people can immediately view and discuss police actions. In Britain a police officer resigned when a video "went viral" showing him breaking the window of a car in order to drag out a driver who had been slow in opening the door. It turned out the man was crippled. An African-American woman in Seattle was shown again and again being flattened by a punch to the face by an officer who had accosted her for jaywalking. That she had been drunk and verbally abusive was not shown. A phone camera recorded an African-American man in New York City dying on the street as a result of being subdued with what appeared to be a prohibited choke hold. The police commissioner himself saw the video and said publicly that if what he saw was confirmed, the officer would be disciplined (New York Times, July 31, 2014).

During the G20 Meeting in London in 2010, Ian Tomlinson, who was walking home from his job and had no connection to the protests which he was passing, was pushed to the ground by riot police officers and assaulted, following which he died. The police initially denied responsibility for the assault, but this denial was very soon belied by the dozens of videos of the incident taken by bystanders on their mobile phones. They were uploaded to the Internet and submitted to the subsequent Independent Police Complaints Commission inquiry that investigated the incident.

In 2015 a police officer in South Carolina in the United States faced murder charges based on allegations that he shot an unarmed man in the back, killing him, as the man was running away from a routine traffic stop for a minor traffic violation. It is questionable whether this would have been identified as a criminal excessive use of force, rather than an act of self-defense, as the officer had at first claimed, if the event had not been videoed by a citizen using his mobile phone. When chiefs as well as the public make determinations from social media, times have indeed changed.

Police departments are themselves increasingly using cameras and social media for crime prevention and investigation, as well as for getting their messages out to the citizenry. CCTV is a prominent example of the former. For their own protection against charges of abuse, officers have begun wearing small video cameras to record problematic encounters—an innovation recently advocated by President Obama as a response to the fatal shooting of an unarmed black man by a white police officer during a protest outside the police station in Ferguson, Missouri.

Investigators are also using the Internet to detect deviant activity, notably child pornography and sex trafficking. They go "under cover" on the net in order to penetrate criminal conspiracies. Finally, some police departments are encouraging the public to use their mobile phones and cameras to report activity that they think requires attention. In effect, neighborhood watch has gone digital, vastly increasing surveillance, even into private spaces that police do not have access to. As another example of the way police are using social media, an Australian commissioner has his own blog, in which he comments every now and again on "What really matters" in his opinion.

Until recently access to these technologies has been slower in India than in our other five countries. A recent survey, for instance, indicated that only 35 percent of the populations in Asian countries had access to the Internet, compared with 70.5 percent in Europe, 88 percent in North America, and 73 percent in Oceana/Australia.[2] A report issued by the World

Bank in 2012 showed that in 2010 83 percent of households in the United States had mobile phones, 77 percent in Canada, 88 percent in Australia, 53 percent in India, 90 percent in New Zealand, and 93 percent in the United Kingdom (Minges and Kimura 2012, 141ff). But a subsequent report indicated that by July 2014, the percentage in India had increased to 70 percent (Srivastava 2014). So we can predict with confidence that these technologies are likely to have similar impact on police governance in all our six countries in the coming years.

Conclusion

In this chapter, we have shown that a number of significant developments with respect to democratic governance generally, as well as the development of various new technologies, have had a significant impact on police governance in our six countries over the last four decades. While India has been the country in which such impact has been the least and slowest so far, there are indications that it is beginning to "catch up" during the second decade of the twenty-first century. We conclude that in those countries in which these developments have been occurring, any program to improve police governance and the chief–political supervisor relationship will necessarily have to take account of them and of the impact that they have had on that relationship.

Notes

1. The original development of these ideas, however, is generally attributed to the Austrian economist and philosopher Friedrich Hayek.
2. See http://www.internetworldstats.com/stats.htm

References

Aucoin, P. 1990. "Administrative Reform in Public Management: Paradigms, Principles, Paradoxes and Pendulums." *Governance* 3(2): 115–37.

Bohman, J. 1996. *Public Deliberation. Pluralism, Complexity, and Democracy.* Cambridge: Cambridge University Press.

Bratton, W. J., and Z. Tumin. 2012. *Collaborate or Perish! Reaching Across Boundaries in a Networked World.* New York: Crown Business.

Dahl, R. 1989. *Democracy and Its Critics.* New Haven, CT: Yale University Press.

Dryzek, J. 2000. *Deliberative Democracy and Beyond: Liberals, Critics, Contestations.* Oxford: Oxford University Press.

Fogelson, R. 1977. *Big City Police.* Cambridge, MA: Harvard University Press.

Gates, D. F., and D. K. Shah. 1992. *Chief: My Life in the LAPD.* New York: Bantam Books.

G4S. 2013. *The G4S Lincolnshire Strategic Partnership–One Year One: Annual Report June 2013.*

Hodgson, J. 2005. *French Criminal Justice: A Comparative Account of the Investigation of Crime in France.* Oxford/Portland, OR: Hart Publishing.

Hood, C. 1995. "The 'New Public Management' in the 1980s: Variations on a Theme." *Accounting, Organisations and Society* 20(2–3):93–109.

Jones, D. S. 2012. *Masters of the Universe: Hayek, Friedman, and the Birth of Neoliberal Politics.* Princeton, NJ: Princeton University Press.

Larner, W. 1997. "A Means to an End: Neo-liberalism and State Processes in New Zealand." *Studies in Political Economy* 47:7–38.

——. 2000. "Neo-liberalism: Policy, Ideology, Governmentality." *Studies in Political Economy* 63:5–25.

——, and W. Walters. 2000. "Privatisation, Governance, Identity: The United Kingdom and New Zealand Compared." *Policy and Politics* 28(3): 361–77

Larson, M. 1979. *The Rise of Professionalism.* Berkeley, CA/ Los Angeles, CA: University of California Press.

Mark, Sir Robert. 1978. *In the Office of Constable: An Autobiography.* London: William Coillins Sons & Co. Ltd.

Martin, J. 1988. *A Profession of Statecraft? Three Essays on Some Current Issues in the New Zealand Public Service.* Wellington, NZ: Victoria University Press.

Minges, M., and K. Kimura. 2012. *Maximizing Mobile, Part II.* Washington, DC: The World Bank.

Osborne, D., and T. Gaebler. 1992. *Reinventing Government: How the Entrepreneurial Spirit Is Transforming the Public Sector*. Reading, MA: Addison-Wesley.

Pateman, C. 1970. *Participation and Democratic Theory*. Cambridge: Cambridge University Press.

Pollitt, Christopher. 1993. *Managerialism and the Public Services: Cuts or Cultural Change in the 1990s?* London: Blackwell Business.

Scott, G., P. Bushnell, and N. Sallee. 1990. "Reform of the Core Public Sector: New Zealand Experience." *Governance* 3(2): 138–67.

Shaw, D. 2013. "Orde Asks May to Review PCC Power to Sack Chief Constables." Accessed September 30, 2015. http://www.bbc.com/news/uk-22907408

Sklansky, David Alan. 2011. "The Persistent Pull of Police Professionalism." In *New Perspectives in Policing*. Washington, DC: National Institute of Justice.

Skogan, Wesley, and Kathleen Frydel, eds. 2004. *Fairness and Effectiveness in Policing: The Evidence*. Washington, DC: National Research Council.

Srivastava, B. 2014. "Mobile and Internet in India 2014." Accessed September 30, 2015. http://dazeinfo.com/2014/07/11/mobile-internet-india-2014-349-million-unique-mobile-phone-users-70-traffic-mobile-india-shining-infographic/

Stenning, P. 1995. "Introduction." In *Accountability for Criminal Justice: Selected Essays*, edited by P. Stenning, 3–14. Toronto: University of Toronto Press.

Stone, C., and J. Travis. 2011. *Toward a New Professionalism in Policing*. Washington, DC: U.S. Department of Justice, Office of Justice Programs. Accessed September 30, 2015. https://research.hks.harvard.edu/publications/digest/citation.aspx?PubId=7776&type=PT&LookupCode=WP

Walker, Samuel. 1977. *A Critical History of Police Reform: The Emergence of Professionalism*. New York: Lexington Books.

———. 2005. *The New World of Police Accountability*. Thousand Oaks, CA: Sage Publications.

Yeatman, A. 1987. "The Concept of Public Management and the Australian State in the 1980s." *Australian Journal of Public Administration* 46(4): 339–56.

9

Improving Police Governance

This book has examined the dynamics of the relationship between senior police executives and elected politicians. It has focused particularly on the question "Who's in charge?," and how the answer to this question is determined in theory and in practice. It has done so narrowly by exploring the nature and frequency of visible disagreement and broadly in terms of the breadth of the "political." It has examined the tactics that chiefs employ in managing the relationship. And it has analyzed the circumstances that are associated across our sample with success and failure.

The time has now come to address the question of reform. What should be done to make police governance more harmonious, and to reduce the likelihood of "boundary disputes," while at the same time serving the public interest? We address the question in three parts:

1. Review the strategies used to manage the relationship between politicians and chiefs and discuss their strengths and weaknesses.
2. Indicate what our research has suggested may be the most promising reforms.
3. Discuss what is necessary to govern police in the public interest.

It is important to underscore that our analysis addresses police governance only in democracies. Police governance in undemocratic countries is far simpler: police do whatever government wants unconstrained by law, morality, or public opinion. Sad to say, police governance of this kind vastly outnumbers the democratic kind. Yearly since 2008, *The Economist* magazine constructs a global democracy index (*Economist* Intelligence Unit, 2013). Their assessment in 2013, covering 163 states and 2 territories and accounting for almost all of the world's population, ranked only 25 countries (15 percent) as "full democracies" (2013). Another 32percent were "flawed democracies." In the world as a whole, democratic police governance is rare.

Devices of Police Governance

Efforts to harmonize political oversight with police independence have involved the following initiatives (Day and Klein 1987; Herbert 2006; Moore et al. 1999; Neyroud 2013; Prenzler 2011; Punch 2006; Sherman 1977):

- Authoritative specification of the respective governance roles of politicians and chiefs
- Creation of appointed boards to supervise police
- Development of memoranda-of-understanding (MOUs)and other types of agreements between politicians and chiefs
- Collaboration by chiefs to articulate and defend professional independence
- Direct election of chiefs

We discuss each of these, recognizing that they do not stand alone but exist in combinations. Authoritative specification of responsibilities through legislation or court decisions may accompany the creation of appointed boards. The clarification of the respective responsibilities may be a crucial task of appointed boards. The presence of appointed boards does not obviate the need for informal agreements between chiefs and politicians. Memoranda-of-understanding may be necessary to make explicit what is not specified in law and legal precedent. Finally, chiefs may organize to influence policy and to protect their governance responsibilities regardless of legislative specification, perhaps, indeed, because of it.

Various mixtures can be seen across our six countries. Australia has had all but the last two; Canada, Old Britain, and New Zealand, all but the last. India has a national law creating the national police structure, but it has no laws at any level that allocate responsibilities between politicians and police. The United States has all in various degrees.

Authoritative Specification

All our countries except India have laws describing in general language the respective roles of politicians and chiefs. These have become most common in recent years in Australia, Britain, Canada, and New Zealand, less so in the United States. The fact that police governance is most dysfunctional in India confirms the importance of role-defining legislation of some sort. In those countries in which this strategy has been adopted, judicial and legislative specifications were initially crude, vague, and left a great deal of room for disputes over interpretation. They typically did not go beyond the general precept that political oversight should be confined to making policy and monitoring performance while operational decisions, including the management of personnel, are the responsibility of police chiefs. Lord Denning's much quoted attempt to define the scope of the political independence of the police, in the *Blackburn* case in 1968, is the most well-known and oft-cited example. It was criticized on the one hand for being too vague, with respect to the activities that were to be independent of politics, and on the other hand overbroad with respect to the extent of their immunity from political accountability. Early attempts at legislative definition were scarcely better.

Over the years, however, spurred on by the recommendations of numerous commissions of inquiry, legislative specification of roles and authorities has become progressively more sophisticated and detailed. The *Victoria Police Act, 2013* in Australia, described in chapter 4, is the most recent and most advanced example of such legislation. What such legislation seeks to achieve is a clear specification of responsibility and authority for different aspects of police governance decision-making—that is, to specify clearly "who's in charge," politicians or police chiefs—with respect to different kinds of decisions. As Stenning (2007, 185–86) noted:

> [I]ndependence may be claimed (or conceded) with respect to *all* or *most* of an organization's or official's decision-making (as is the case generally, for instance, with judicial independence), or with respect to only certain (more or less clearly specified) areas of decision-making.

In this regard, it may be helpful, in discussing the *scope* of police independence, to differentiate the following eight subjects of decision-making:

1. Resourcing—how much, and what kinds of, funds, equipment, staffing, etc. will be made available to an organization
2. Appointments—chiefs, deputy chiefs, and assistant chiefs
3. Organizational structure and management—how the organization will be structured, organized, and managed
4. Organizational policies—general policies that the organization will be expected to adhere to in its operations
5. Priority setting—the determination of priorities with respect to how the resources of the organization will be deployed
6. Deployment—how the organization will deploy the resources available to it, either generally or in particular circumstances
7. Appointments and promotions—all ranks below Assistant Chief
8. Specific operational decision-making—how a particular operation will be handled and managed

The accepted norm in most common law jurisdictions is now that the *least* police independence is conceded with respect to decisions at the upper end of the list, and the *most* for those at the lower end of the list. There is virtually no disagreement, for instance, in most jurisdictions that decisions about overall resourcing and budgets (type 1) and appointments to most or all of the top three ranks (type 2) are the ultimate prerogative of governments. Similarly, there is virtually no disagreement that appointments and promotions to lower ranks (type 7) and specific individual operational decisions (type 8) should be the exclusive preserve of the police. They are the sacrosanct areas of police responsibility, not to be "interfered" with or influenced by politicians.

With respect to the decisions between these two extremes (types 3-6), there has been no such consensus. Responsibility is more contentious, and the distributions of responsibility between politicians and chiefs for these kinds of decisions vary quite considerably from one jurisdiction to another and often vary over time within any one jurisdiction. They are typically the subject of ad hoc negotiation between the government and a newly appointed chief. This is unsatisfactory for two reasons. In the first place, chiefs and their political supervisors do not have equal power in such negotiations. A prospective chief who does not accept the distribution proposed by the government simply does not get appointed; a chief who does not adhere to it while in office can be dismissed or not have his or her contract renewed. Secondly, leaving these matters to re-negotiation every time a new police chief or a new political supervisor is appointed risks an endless uncertainty and lack of continuity in the police chief–political supervisor relationship.

Legislative specification has been a strategy to avoid, or at least reduce, this uncertainty and lack of continuity, and provide established and clear "ground rules" for any negotiation that may still be required to deal with details of interpretation in practice—in short, to reduce the likelihood of major "boundary disputes" between chiefs and their political supervisors. The 2013 legislation in Victoria, for instance, allocates responsibility and authority for each of the eight decision types noted above between the police minister and the chief commissioner. Ultimate authority for decision types 1, 4, and 5 is given to the minister, while ultimate authority with respect to decision types 3, 6, 7, and 8 is given to the chief commissioner. With respect to type 2 decisions, the minister has ultimate authority with respect to the appointment of a chief commissioner and deputy commissioners (although the minister is required to consult with the chief commissioner before appointing deputy commissioners), and the chief commissioner is given the exclusive authority to appoint assistant commissioners.

Even with such detailed allocation of responsibilities there will still be room for, and a need for, some negotiation with respect to matters that the allocation does not clearly specify (e.g., does ministerial responsibility for decisions concerning "equipment" include authority to determine exactly what kinds of firearms the police may carry?). The intended effect of the legislation is to reduce this need as much as possible so that major disputes about responsibility and authority are much less likely to arise.

The success of any legislative specification in achieving clarity depends on the care with which it is drafted and the extent to which vague and ambiguous terminology which can give rise to disputes is avoided. The recent British legislation establishing Police and Crime Commissioners, for example, is quite deficient in this respect. It refers to the "operational independence" of chief constables without specifying what this entails. To make matters worse, the Policing Protocol Order issued by the Home Secretary pursuant to Section 79 of the legislation contradicts the provision in the legislation concerning a chief constable's exclusive authority with respect to the "direction and control of the Force and day-to-day management of such force assets" by adding the qualifying words "as agreed by the PCC." Many chief constables understandably have expressed concern that this will increase rather than reduce the likelihood of disputes between chief constables and their PCC's since it introduces uncertainty over the previously accepted understanding of the scope of chief constables' political independence.

Legislative specification, therefore, is not the "silver bullet" that will eliminate all possible opportunities for disagreement between chiefs and their political supervisors. But it does offer the possibility of reducing such disagreements and providing a clearer basis for resolving them when they do arise. Our interviewees in those countries in which such legislative specification has been adopted (notably in New Zealand and some Australian jurisdictions), and in some Canadian jurisdictions (notably Ontario), have attested to its effectiveness. Our research suggests that it is probably no coincidence that serious disputes are most common in India where such legislation does not exist and in the United States where it does, largely at state levels, but is vague and couched in generalities.

The role-allocation problem has been looked at in another way in the United States. The issue is often described there as balancing political oversight with police professionalism rather than as a matter of "police independence." The notion is that police have special skills in making the judgments required for effective policing that can only be learned through experience. Police, it is argued, are like doctors, airplane pilots, civil engineers, plumbers, and auto mechanics in that hands-on decisions should not be overruled by amateurs. On this reckoning, then, what decisions should be the exclusive prerogative of "professional" police chiefs? What unique experience-based skills do police have?

Michael Brogden, one of the few scholars to address this issue, listed the following (1982, 236):

- Legality of actions
- Judicial knowledge of the prosecution process
- Strategies and tactics of law enforcement
- Use of resources
- Equity in the application of law

This is obviously a generous view of what should be sacrosanct to police judgment. It enlarges the independence of police chiefs considerably at the expense of collaborating with politicians. It is also out-of-date. Public opinion, and to some extent police opinion, has shifted sharply against so broad a view of police expertise. This is certainly true with respect to judgments about equity in law enforcement, strategies of law enforcement, and the use of resources. It is not an exaggeration to say that in today's climate of opinion, the only decisions that would be left exclusively to chiefs if based on an assessment of professional skills would be the tactics employed in actions occurring in the field. Even there, however, police have increasingly accepted the view that research is needed in order to determine what strategies and tactics work best.

Professionalism is no longer accepted as a strong argument for police autonomy. It is valued today not out of respect for police judgment but because of the fear of partisanship at the expense of the public interest and to encourage respect from citizens. Concern about the respective roles of politicians and police today has more to do with preventing partisan encroachment and upholding the rule of law than raising the quality of decisions.

Appointed Boards

Boards with general governance responsibilities have been interposed between supervising politicians and chiefs in

some of our six countries. They are commonly given responsibility for making policy, monitoring police performance,
and appointing chiefs. At present, however, the only one of
our six countries in which such boards are commonplace
is Canada, and then only for the governance of municipal
and regional police services. Boards that were established to
govern major city police forces in the United States in the
nineteenth century were mostly eventually abolished. A few
governance boards still exist in the United States, however,
but are very controversial. The radically decentralized structure of US policing also limits their usefulness. The United
States has approximately 17,000 police forces (Maguire and
Pastore 2008, 28, Table 1). According to the Bureau of Justice
Statistics, about half of all agencies employed fewer than ten
full-time officers (Reaves 2011). In jurisdictions this small
appointment of boards would be impractical and perhaps
unnecessary. The US solution to the political supervision
problem has been to create city managers—appointed fixed-
term administrators who supervise all municipal services.
Their powers vary considerably across the country. For
example, some do and some do not appoint chiefs. Even
when they do, it is always with the approval of mayors and
city councils. City managers serve the same function as
appointed boards—attenuating political directiveness while
ensuring accountability.

The Watch Committees which existed in Old Britain
were replaced with Police Authorities in 1964, which in turn
were abolished and replaced with elected Police and Crime
Commissioners in 2011. A Police Board was established to
govern the New South Wales Police Service in 1983, but was
abolished thirteen years later. A similar Board was established
to govern the Victoria Police in 1992, but was abolished seven
years later. A proposal for such a board was put forward in a
discussion paper in South Australia in 1992 (Lawson 1992),
but it was never established. No other Australian jurisdiction

has had such a board, nor has New Zealand. The establishment of boards in the Indian states was recommended by the
National Police Commission in 1979 and the implementation
of this proposal was mandated by the Indian Supreme Court
in 2006. Despite the court order, few states have created them.

Notwithstanding these rejections of Police Boards in five
of our six countries, several of our interviewees (especially
in Canada and Britain) expressed support for such boards.[1]
There are two advantages to such boards. First, they provide
a place to discuss allocations of responsibilities apart from
direct discussions between the political supervisors and police
chiefs themselves. In effect, they serve as a buffer between
the two by allowing negotiations to occur in the presence of
a referee. Second, because they contain representatives of the
public, people who are neither politicians nor police, they
allow direct public representation in the oversight process.

Governance boards are most typically composed of some
combination of locally elected politicians and non-elected
"independent" appointees, whether chosen by local governments or appointed by more senior-level governments. Such
non-elected appointees are usually selected on the basis of
interest, expertise, or community representativeness. In
most, but by no means all, cases elected persons make up the
majority of the membership of governing boards, although
sometimes only by one vote. Boards thus combine political
representation with some measure of political independence.

Memoranda-of-Understanding and Other Negotiated Agreements

With or without legislation, judicial decisions, and
boards, politicians and chiefs may develop their own agreements about their respective prerogatives. Memoranda-
of-understanding appear to be more common in the United
States than elsewhere in our sample. This may be because
disagreements about respective responsibilities are more

common in the United States. Since the introduction of
Police and Crime Commissioners in New Britain, at least
one police area (North Yorkshire) has seen the promulgation
of an MOU between the PCC and the chief constable with
a view to specifying their relationship more clearly than the
legislation has done.[2] MOUs represent an ad hoc solution
to a common problem. The decision to negotiate one can
be problematic: MOUs may solve anticipated disagreements
about responsibilities but they may also prompt discussions
about problems that will never arise. It may sometimes
be better to let sleeping dogs lie. With or without formal
MOUs, frank discussions about respective responsibilities
may become necessary in any jurisdiction.

The advent of neoliberalism and the New Public
Management, discussed in chapter 8, led to other kinds
of agreements—purchase agreements, performance agreements, police commissioner contracts, and detailed position
descriptions—which specify more clearly the responsibilities,
authorities, and accountabilities of chiefs and their political
supervisors. Like MOUs these various agreements vary among
jurisdictions and over time.

Coordination among Chiefs

Because decisions about policy can so profoundly affect
operations, police chiefs have sought ways to insert a strong,
professional voice in policy making. They are handicapped
in doing so. Chiefs are responsible for faithfully implementing policy as formulated and not to "politic" about it. The
price of operational independence is avoidance of political
advocacy. The problem with this is that chiefs have valuable
experience that may be in the public interest to share.

One solution adopted by chiefs has been to organize
an "industry" point of view in policy discussions. The
Association of Chief Police Officers (ACPO) in Britain has

been the most successful example of this. That may have changed, however, when the Conservative government created directly elected Police and Crime Commissioners in 2011 and replaced ACPO with a National Police Chiefs' Council in 2015. So Britain no longer has Police Boards with direct governing authority but does still have an organized professional police voice.

A police voice has been developed piecemeal over time through voluntary associations of police in other countries, such as the Canadian Association of Chiefs of Police (CACP–Marquis 1993), the International Association of Chiefs of Police in the United States (IACP), and the American Major-City Chiefs Association. India has a nationally selected and trained officer corps—the Indian Police Service (IPS)—that might serve this purpose but has never tried to do so. In all six countries, chiefs regularly meet together in various forums to discuss specific policy issues and, less often, announce their positions. In Australia and New Zealand this is the Australia New Zealand Policing Advisory Agency ANZPAA), established by the commissioners in both countries.

Direct Elections

The Gordian Knot of police governance may be cut by directly electing police chiefs, thereby combining the roles of politician and chief. This occurs only in the United States with elected county sheriffs, and reflects a tradition for other senior criminal justice officials (including prosecutors and judges) to be directly elected rather than appointed. Counties are a layer of government larger than municipalities and smaller than states. US sheriffs speak enthusiastically about the simplicity of this arrangement. By virtue of elections, they are directly accountable to the public for all aspects of policing, from policy formulation to tactical command. As one sheriff we interviewed said,

burying chiefs under layers of elected and unelected supervisors "does not improve the odds of good decision-making.
But having an elected CEO gives that CEO an independent
voice on the issues."

The new Police and Crime Commissioners in Britain are
a hybrid of direct election. Although enjoined by a Home
Office protocol (2011) not to interfere in operational matters, the PCCs have authority to make policy and hold chief
constables accountable. However, unlike US sheriffs, they
are not police officers. They do not have law enforcement
powers. The Home Office's guidance for harmonizing this
division of labor with chief constables, discussed earlier, is
unfortunately as ambiguous and contestable as under the
tripartite system it replaced.[3]

While direct election of chief law enforcement officers
simplifies police governance by combining politics and management in one person, it exposes policing to majoritarian
politics. Complex issues of law enforcement often become
unrealistically simplified —"sloganized"—during elections.
The electoral stump is rarely a place to explore subtle issues
of law, morality, and best practice. The endorsement of direct
elections by US sheriffs may reflect administrative convenience more than the public interest. Tugs-of-war between
elected political overseers and professional police managers
can be awkward, but they are necessary for negotiating the
achievement of co-equal sets of objectives.

Improving Police Governance

Based on our analysis of police governance in six democratic countries, we draw three conclusions about how
disruptive and unproductive disputes between politicians
and chiefs may be reduced, namely, by legislative stipulation, preparatory training for chiefs and politicians at the
time of appointment, and the establishment of police-
governing boards.

Legislative Specification

Four of the countries that we have studied (Australia, Britain, Canada, and New Zealand) have during the last three decades introduced progressively more detailed legislation delineating the respective police governance responsibilities of politicians and police chiefs, and the desired relationships between them. The provisions of the 2013 Victorian legislation in Australia, which we described in some detail in chapter 4, represent both the most recent and the most comprehensive of these legislative prescriptions. In many cases this has been in response to specific and serious instances of a breakdown in these relationships, and on the recommendations of inquiries that have been set up to examine them, with a view to making such ruptures less likely in the future.

One of the advantages of legislative stipulation of the respective roles of chiefs and their political supervisors is that by establishing a legally enforceable delineation of these, it reduces the necessity as well as the authorization for chiefs and their political supervisors to re-negotiate these from scratch whenever a new chief or political supervisor is appointed. In other words, it provides an established and accepted benchmark from which the finer details of the relationship can be worked out and agreed upon and adjustments made as circumstances are thought to require. In this way it promotes stability and continuity in the chief–political supervisor relationship. If circumstances change such that the existing legislative allocation of responsibilities and authorities are no longer considered appropriate, the legislation can be amended. That, of course, cannot always be done easily or quickly, but that may not be a bad thing if the legislative process provides an opportunity for careful consideration and public discussion and input.

The chiefs whom we interviewed in Australia, Britain, and New Zealand were almost unanimous in asserting that this kind of legislative specification had not only clarified the respective authority and responsibilities of police chiefs and the politicians to whom they are politically accountable, but had also increased the scope of both the political supervision over the police and the political accountability of chiefs. As we explained in chapter 8, this reflected changed attitudes toward democratic governance and management of public services. Although some of our interviewees expressed concern that this amounted to an undesirable increased "politicization" of policing, many (especially in Australia) also acknowledged that it had had a beneficial effect in reducing the frequency of serious disputes between chiefs and the politicians to whom they are accountable.[4]

Legislative specification of roles and responsibilities is certainly not a panacea in this respect. Our research suggests, however, that the claim that it reduces serious disputes between chiefs and their political supervisors has been borne out by recent experience in those countries where such legislative specification has been introduced.

Preparation of Chiefs and Politicians at the Time of Appointment

Our interviewees in all of the six countries that we studied supported the idea that on being nominated to their posts, supervising politicians and chiefs need to be educated in the challenges that democratic governance involves. Chiefs acknowledge that they have generally not been well prepared for the complexity of their new responsibilities. As one scholar has observed, "Few municipal functions are simultaneously as sensitive and as seemingly insensitive to the citizenry, as routine and as unpredictable, as rule-bound and as discretionary, as supervised by external oversight and as unsupervisable (even invisible) in detail, as is policing" (Andrews 1985). For most politicians and chiefs, the exigencies and complexities of governance have had to be learned on the job after appointment.

Remedial action, however, has been uneven. The need has been addressed most concertedly in Old and New Britain where candidates for promotion to senior command ranks (assistant, deputy, and chief constable) are selected by the National Assessment Centre and are then required to attend the commanders' course at Bramshill Police College (now re-named the National Police College). Although the course provides an occasion for the tactics of political management to be discussed, most attention seems to have gone to technical matters of budgeting, organization, and crime prevention. Australia is also developing courses for senior managers at the Australian Institute of Police Management at Manley, New South Wales. They are not, however, mandatory for promotable officers. Senior police officers from New Zealand also participate in these courses.

India has recently required advanced training for both mid-career and most senior ranked officers at its National Police Academy in Hyderabad. The problem of police interference is fully recognized in this course but suggestions for managing it are rarely discussed. Canada has a Senior Command Course at the Canadian Police College. Some US officers may attend the National Executive Institute run by the FBI. That, plus a short seminar for senior police officers by the Police Executive Research Forum, is all that is offered in the United States. In most of these programs issues of police governance in democracies are not seriously examined.

Our research suggests that newly appointed supervising politicians and chiefs should be provided with a short, formal orientation to, or briefing about, the governance relationship, as is provided in several Canadian jurisdictions and in New Zealand. Two days would probably be sufficient, provided it focuses on the problematics of the relationship and not on technical details of administration and operations. Training should feature discussions led by skilled facilitators who are familiar with the problems that customarily arise. Former chiefs might also be enrolled to share their experiences. Such training must be interactive, featuring discussion and selective role-playing. Case studies of good and bad governance should be presented. Although presentations by serving and retired politicians and chiefs can be useful, it would be helpful if facilitators were from other professional worlds, such as academia or non-governmental organizations.

The objective of the training should be to teach the participants how to play their roles without becoming unreasonable and personal. It should provide an opportunity to learn the wisdom in the observation that "accountability is all about the social and political processes involved in developing an agreed language of discourse about how to judge conduct" (Day and Klein 1987, 56). In short, participants should learn how to negotiate in a principled but collaborative way. Achieving democratic police governance is a process. Making it work well requires education in the process.

Appointed Boards

Our research suggests that the creation of appointed boards situated between elected politicians and chiefs can be effective in reducing serious disagreements in police governance. Evidence for this comes from the performance of Police Services Boards in Canada and Police Authorities in Old Britain.

The unique advantage of Police Boards is that they can assume responsibility for defining the boundary between political and police authority. Politicians may still ask for or suggest particular courses of actions, but police can refuse with greater impunity and have the benefit of the participation of nonpartisan neutral board members in the discussion.

Having a board as the political supervisor, however, does not guarantee that dysfunctional disputes will not arise, for several reasons. The proportion of elected to non-elected members can be controversial, as is the representativeness of appointed members. Furthermore, members, both political and independent, may be inexperienced in police matters. While it is important to hear from representative members of the public, independent members may be treated as amateurs among experienced police and political heavyweights. They are often fully employed elsewhere and cannot devote sufficient time to their responsibilities as board members. Finally, the creation of a local board with a majority of members who are politicians may do no more than re-locate the police–politician relationship (e.g., from a provincial to a municipal level) without actually ameliorating it.

In order for boards to fulfill their responsibilities of making policy, monitoring performance, mediating disputes, and hiring and firing chiefs, they must be carefully constructed and adequately supported. Specifically, boards require:

- Independence from partisan control
- Adequate powers to inquire
- Expertise in police matters, by appointment or staffing
- An obligation to publicly report about the condition of the police

It must be recognized, however, that appointed boards, particularly those with a majority of non-elected members, have been rejected as incompatible with principles of democratic police governance and accountability in some of the jurisdictions that we have studied. This has notably been the case in Australia, where such boards have been proposed and/or introduced in three states and either proposals have been rejected or boards that have been established have soon been abolished, with a return to more traditional ministerial responsibility. In Britain, the old Police Authorities were criticized for not representing sufficiently the views of local communities about police priorities and behavior. This was the ostensible justification for replacing them with directly elected local Police and Crime Commissioners, supported and monitored by local advisory Police and Crime Panels. Boards are also not considered a practically viable option in countries, such as the United States, which have large numbers of very small police departments, and have been rejected as unsuitable for the large provincial/state and federal police services in Canada. So the establishment of such boards may not be a feasible strategy to reduce police chief–political supervisor disputes in all democratic countries.

Governing in the Public Interest

Albert O. Hirschmann (1970) wrote an influential book in which he argued that people who work in large organizations have three options when confronted with directives from superiors. They can quit, argue within for a change in policy, or comply. He called these Exit, Voice, and Loyalty. Instructively, this analysis does not apply to the choices police chiefs face, even though they are in formally subordinate positions. Police chiefs are enjoined by democratic theory to be loyal not only to representative government but to a set of normative principles, namely, law, human rights, and professional experience represented by "best practice." The dilemma for chiefs is that they have multiple loyalties. They must continually determine not just who's in charge, but who *should be* in charge.

Ever since responsibility for the police was transferred from magistrates to elected politicians in common law jurisdictions in the nineteenth century, there has been a concern to ensure some separation between policing and politics. On the one hand, partisan political "meddling" in specific police operations and decisions with respect to the application of the law in individual cases (what the British Royal Commission report in 1962 referred to as "quasi-judicial" decisions) threatens to undermine the rule of law, and perceptions of the police as fair and impartial. At the other end of the governance spectrum, excessive involvement of the police in politics similarly threatens their perceived legitimacy as fair and impartial enforcers of the law. So it is with good reason that in all of the six countries that we have studied, there is a consensus that the ultimate authority to make decisions should be allocated exclusively to politicians at the extreme policy end of the spectrum and to police at the extreme operational end of the spectrum.

Between these two "sacrosanct" extremes, however, lies a wide range of governance decisions with respect to which a bright line between "policy" and "operations" cannot be drawn—decisions which may be perceived as primarily policy decisions have operational impacts, and decisions that may be perceived as primarily operational have policy implications. Indeed if there were not such links between policy and operations, policies would be useless.

It is with respect to these non-sacrosanct decisions that democratic governance works best to ensure the public interest, provided it is characterized by mutual consultation between politicians and police and allows a genuine opportunity for public discussion and input. As we noted in chapter 5, the 2011 Police Reform and Social Responsibility Act in Britain provides a good example of how a requirement for this can be legislatively stipulated.

Legislative stipulation, however, is subject to interpretation. Conditions on the ground change that were not anticipated either in legislation or policy directives. Some disputes may be resolved by courts. Others will generate disputes about the content of the customarily "sacrosanct" extremes, as well as in the "negotiable middle" despite the specifications of legislation. For these reasons, the respective prerogatives of politicians and chiefs everywhere will from time to time need adjustment. India today, for example, needs less direct political control. Conversely, the British government thought in 2011 that police governance needed a greater measure of direct, local accountability and thus instituted elected Police and Crime Commissioners. Australia seems more concerned at the moment with adding accountability than limiting political direction. Americans seem to be concerned equally about partisan interference and police accountability. They want more accountability but not under political auspices.

The fundamental fact is that police governance is unavoidably political (Reiner 1991). The need for negotiation cannot be settled once and for all through formal arrangements or clever management. Relations between politicians and chiefs are a perpetual dance, forward and back. There may be rest periods, but neither can permanently sit it out.

In order to be responsive to the public interest, therefore, discussions about the distributions of authority between politicians and chiefs should not begin with insistence on particular distributions. It should begin with a willingness to examine, discuss, and decide how the public interest is best served. The mantra of "operational independence" is of limited value because any "balance" is usually issue specific and temporary. Police governance is not owned by either politicians or chiefs. Rather, it is shared. William G. Bowen and Eugene M. Tobin came to the same conclusion about the distribution of authority between academic administrators and faculty (2014). Pleading "academic freedom," faculties often insist on the authority to make certain kinds of decisions independent of the administration's judgment, in just the way police chiefs use "operational independence" to fend off political direction. In order to be successful, however, governance in law enforcement, as in universities, must be shared according to the requirements of issues and exigencies of the moment, rather than according to rigid formulas about turf.

To serve the public interest, shared governance in policing must reflect the obligation to achieve something greater than mutual accommodations of authority. One hopes, of course, that governance in private sector contexts will also serve the public interest, but accountability in those institutions stops with trustees and shareholders through boards of directors. In the public sector, however, executives such as police chiefs, as well as politicians, must act in a public interest which is not owned by them. Convenient, even comfortable, governance in policing is not an end in itself. It must achieve goals that neither politicians nor chiefs, working separately or together, can be allowed exclusive authority to judge.

Many of our police chief interviewees stressed the importance of such co-operation and consultation for a successful, dispute-free relationship with their political supervisors, rather than a rigid defense of their decision-making "turf," except in the case of those purely operational decisions allocated exclusively to police. As one chief commented, "You can't have successful police governance if the chief and his or her political supervisor are constantly at war with each other." The relationship requires a high level of "give and take" with respect to decisions, especially those that are not in the "sacrosanct" categories, and recognition of the practical and political constraints within which each party must function.

In order to ensure that shared governance works in the public interest, the inevitable negotiations, explicit or implied, between politicians and chiefs should be made with input from the public. This occurs, of course, with respect to the enactment of legislation through elected representatives of the public. This may be inadequate because it does not reflect the specifics of issues or contexts. Legislative hearings, if they are timely, can be very helpful for just these reasons. But local voices need to be heard wherever decisions about distributions of authority are made, especially where local knowledge is crucial. Police Boards provide another venue for this kind of public involvement. This does not mean that all negotiations between politicians and chiefs must be conducted in a public forum. It does mean, however, that the importance of negotiations must be recognized and the manner in which they are conducted should become a matter of public discourse. The public, as well as politicians and chiefs, should be educated in the necessity of these negotiations. Advance training for politicians and chiefs should focus on this.

In this process, the phrase "operational independence" retains some usefulness. It can remind politicians, police, and the public that perspectives matter and, when they differ, should be openly acknowledged and if possible reconciled. "Operational independence" should be thought of as a flag, not a recipe. When its content becomes controversial, the public needs to understand what is at stake and to participate in the shaping of a new balance.

Finally, under any institutional model for moderating disagreements between politicians and chiefs, governments must ensure the presence of a politically independent judiciary. This is essential for ensuring adherence to law and its equal application among jurisdictions. The rule of law is fundamental to democratic government. Its ultimate custodian is the judiciary.

Conclusion

After reviewing the strengths and weaknesses of the strategies of police governance in the six countries we studied, we have concluded that legislative stipulation of respective police/political roles, creating police boards, and providing education for politicians and chiefs in managing the governance relationship would help significantly to reduce dysfunction in the relationship. At the same time, we suggest that a new perspective on the practice of police governance is needed. It would recognize the inevitability of negotiation between police and politicians as conditions change. Both have a responsibility larger than their own professional interests. Police governance is shared, but it needs to be shared with a difference. Legislative and judicial specification will, of course, always be needed. But police governance should also be negotiated where it is informed by the particularities of localities, including the perspectives of different publics.

The challenge for police government in democratic countries is to develop appropriate devices to reflect this perspective. Sharing governance close to the needs of localities will be messy and sometimes inconvenient. It is certainly political. It is also the essence of democratic government.

Notes

1. Several of the police chiefs whom Caless interviewed, however, complained of improper interference in operation matters by Police Authorities that were their political supervisors at the time (Caless 2011, chap. 4). He reported that 70% of his interviewees were "negative about Police Authorities" (p. 120).

2. See http://www.northyorkshire-pcc.gov.uk/about/who-we-are/Julia-mulligan/memorandum-of-undersanding.

3. The Protocol can be accessed online at https://www.gov.uk/government/uploads/system/uploads/attachment_data/file/117474/policing-protocol-order.pdf. For a more detailed discussion of it, see chapter 5.

4. Two former New Zealand Commissioners, in testimony before parliamentary committee hearings on the 2008 *Policing Bill,* expressed strong opposition to these provisions on the ground of "politicization."

References

Andrews, A. H., Jr. 1985. "Structuring the Political Independence of the Police Chief." In *Police leadership in America*, edited by W. A. Geller, Chap. 1, pp. 5–19. New York: ABA and Praeger.

Bowen, W. G. 2008. *The Board Book: An Insider's Guide for Directors and Trustees*. New York: W.W. Norton and Company.

Brogden, M. 1982. *The Police: Autonomy and Consent*. London: Academic Press.

Caless, B. 2011. *Policing at the Top: The Roles, Values and Attitudes of Chief Police Officers*. Bristol: The Policy Press.

Day, P., and Klein, R. 1987. *Accountabilities: Five Public Services*. London: Tavistock Publications.

Economist Intelligence Unit. 2013. *The Economist*. Online.

Herbert, S. 2006. "Tangled Up in Blue: Conflicting Paths to Police Legitimacy." *Theoretical Criminology* 10 (4): 481–504.

Hirschman, Albert O. 1970. *Exit, Voice, and Loyalty: Responses to Decline in Firms, Organizations, and States*. Cambridge, MA: Harvard University Press.

Lawson, T. 1992. *Report to Heads of Agencies Committee on Establishment of a Police Board in South Australia*. South Australian Attorney-General's Department, unpublished report.

Maguire, K., and Pastore, A. 2008. *Sourcebook of Criminal Justice Statistics*. Albany, NY: Hindelang Criminal Justice Research Center.

Marquis, G. 1993. *Policing Canada's Century: A History of the Canadian Association of Chiefs of Police*. Toronto, ON: University of Toronto Press.

Moore, M. H., Thatcher, D., Hartmann, F. X., and Coles, C. 1999. *Case Studies of the Transformation of Police Departments: A Cross-site Analysis*. Washington, DC: Urban Institute Press.

Neyroud, P. 2013. The Governance, Accountability, Oversight and Regulation of the Police. Powerpoint presentation from a lecture to the MCTC, National Police Academy, Hyderabad, India.

Prenzler, T. 2011. "The Evolution of Police Oversight in Australia." *Policing and Society* 21 (3): 284–303.

Punch, M., with J. Markam. March 16-17, 2006. "Embracing Accountability." Draft paper for the Columbia/King's College workshop on policing, democracy, and the rule of law, London.

Reaves, B. 2011. *Census of State and Local Law Enforcement Agencies 2008*. Washington, DC: Bureau of Justice Statistics, Department of Justice.

Reiner, Robert. 1991. *Chief Constables: Bobbies, Bosses, or Bureaucrats*. London: Oxford University Press.

Sherman, L. W. 1977. "Police Corruption Control: Environmental Context Versus Organizational Policy." In *Police and Society*, edited by D. H. Bayley, Chap. 5, pp. 107–26. Beverly Hills, CA: Sage.

Stenning, P. 1981. *Police Commissions and Boards in Canada*. Toronto, ON: Centre of Criminology, University of Toronto.

———. 2007. "The Idea of the Political 'Independence' of the Police: International Interpretations and Experiences." In *Police and Government Relations: Who's Calling the Shots?*, edited by M. Beare and T. Murray, 183–256. Toronto: University of Toronto Press.

Index